Something Old Something New

What You Didn't Know About
Wedding Ceremonies,
Celebrations & Customs

Vera Lee

CASABLANCA PRESS
A DIVISION OF SOURCEBOOKS, INC.
Naperville, IL

Published by: Sourcebooks, Inc.
P.O. Box 372, Naperville, Illinois, 60566
(630) 961-3900
FAX: (630) 961-2618

"A Word to Husbands" from *Marriage Lines: Notes Of A Student Husband* by Ogden
Nash. Copyright © 1962, 1964 by Ogden Nash. Reprinted by permission of Little,
Brown and Company.

Lyrics to the song "Alma" by Tom Lehrer. Copyright © 1965 by Tom Lehrer. Used
by permission.

The Lives and Times of Archy and Mehitabel by Don Marquis. Copyright © 1927,
1930, 1933, 1935, 1950 by Doubleday, a Division of Bantam, Doubleday, Dell
Publishing Group, Inc. Used by permission of Doubleday.

Library of Congress Cataloging-in-Publication Data

Lee, Vera.
    Something old, something new : what you didn't know about wedding
ceremonies, celebrations and customs / by Vera Lee.
        p.   cm.
Includes bibliographical references.
ISBN 1-57071-002-3 : $14.95 (hc); 1-57071-148-8 : $9.95 (pap)
1. Marriage customs and rites.   I. Title.
GT2665.L44   1994
392' .5—dc20   94–235
                                                        CIP

Printed and bound in the United States of America
Paperback Edition
10 9 8 7 6 5 4 3 2 1

To Sarah and Sophie,

with love and kisses

from Nunski.

Table of Contents

vii

Acknowledgments

First a word of warm thanks to family, friends and acquaintances who pointed me to precious sources of wedding trivia, contributed information or gave me enthusiastic support.

Gratitude to Amanda and Conrad Gees, authors Greg Godek, Anne Baker and Edith Schwartz and publisher Jane Daniel, who took time from her crammed schedule to read this manuscript at the eleventh hour.

Many thanks also to actress Ilona Ricardo, Madiha Elbassiony, Dr. Nathan Schneider, Demetrios Tsoumbanos, Mark Altbush, William Cody, Rebecca Arnoldi, Lucienne Davidson, Uthai Jamsri, Pam Kessler, Joseph Longtin, Mo Marikar and Charlotte Whiting. And a sincere salute to those kind, unidentified foreign nationals I accosted in the street or elsewhere, who graciously provided corroboration or supplemental information for my research.

Some highly useful centers of information for this book were the Harvard College libraries (Widener, Schlesinger and Tozzer Anthropological Library), Boston College libraries (O'Neill and Burns) and assorted public libraries in the area.

Introduction: What Makes a Wedding?

"Marriage is a science."

–Honoré de Balzac

What is it that gets you from single to spliced? A ring placed on a finger? Assembled guests sitting all in a row? The kiss at the altar? Most people believe it's the ceremony itself, the exchange of vows and those magic words, "I now pronounce you man and wife." But as a matter of fact, today's wedding ritual is a fairly recent invention. Before 1547—when the Catholic Church set forth its sacraments in the Council of Trent—the wedding story was very different indeed.

In early times, couples simply chose each other and began living together as spouses. Or they set up housekeeping once their marriage was arranged by the head of a tribe or some other figure of authority. They needed no rings, no special wedding clothes, no vows to love, honor or cherish to consider themselves married. In fact, what usually sealed the pact wasn't a wedding at all, but an official engagement or "betrothal": a promise—made before witnesses—to live as man and wife.

Still, people have always liked to celebrate their rites of passage with a bit of ceremony—some sort of pomp and circumstance to herald important events. And what event could be more important than committing yourself to a lifetime partner? So all over the planet different societies developed an endless variety of rituals to consecrate the day and to orchestrate the union of bride and groom.

Some have broken bread over the bride's head or combed her hair in public. Others have had the groom leave an animal carcass at her door. Most communities have organized processions to the bride's house, and nearly all of them have surrounded the new couple with a host of deeply entrenched superstitions.

Those of us who get most of our wedding information from Amy Vanderbilt, Martha Stewart or *Bride's Magazine* may find such customs and popular beliefs quaint or exotic. Yet a whole spectrum of ancient wedding traditions continues to survive even today—and not only in remote rural villages overseas. As we shall see, these age-old practices and superstitions form the very basis of our own modern wedding rites.

The following pages will provide the curious with a broad medley of marriage customs, past and present, from all over the world.

Prelude: The Courting Game

"My most brilliant achievement was...to persuade my wife to marry me."

–Winston Churchill

"He got down, all trembly, on one knee and asked me to be his wife. I said yes. There's a point when all this dignity and stuff get in the way of destiny."

–Rita Dove,
Through the Ivory Gate

In nineteenth-century America, a young man courting a maiden was labelled her "spark." People called kissing and hugging "sparking"— perhaps from all that friction.

Cuddling couples early in the twentieth century would "spoon" (under the moon in June). Other terms for those amorous activities: "playing gitchy" or "slap and tickle."

They called it "necking" from the 1920s through the 1950s. "Petting" referred to heavier duty fondling, rather than just plain hugs and kisses. But of course nice girls didn't admit to doing that.

Did our forefathers really "bundle"? Yes, indeed— from earliest colonial days until the nineteenth century. When a young lad "came a-courting," especially in winter time, the girl's parents would let him stay overnight in the same bed as their daughter, provided they both kept some clothes on or bundled up in bedcovers.

Bundling made lots of sense at the time. The family didn't have to burn precious wood in the evening, the boy wasn't obliged to walk long miles home on cold nights and parents could have their space to themselves and sleep in peace.

Although bundling boards (supposedly separating the bedded couple) came into fashion after the Revolution, many a bride arrived at the altar in a family way. This didn't seem to bother people, though, provided the erring couple wound up married.

Verses from a 1786 ballad in favor of bundling:

> "Nature's request is give me rest,
> Our bodies seek repose.
> Night is the time and 'tis no crime
> To bundle in our cloaths.

> "Since in a bed, a man and maid
> May bundle and be chaste:

It doth no good to burn up wood,
It is a needless waste."

Dating didn't really catch on in the U.S. until after World War I. Before that a young man usually courted a miss in her own parlor, sometimes embarrassingly within sight of her parents. The automobile got couples out of the house and to dances, restaurants and theater—not to mention country lanes. (But the new dating system also put a strain on most men's wallets.)

In most countries LOVE has had very little to do with marriage. Parents arranged marriages, and many still arrange them today in Asia, Africa and other parts of the world. In fact, some families promise sons and daughters to each other when the children are still in their infancy (cradle betrothal) or even fetuses, providing the gender works out satisfactorily.

Benazir Bhutto's marriage was arranged by her mother in 1987, one year before she became Prime

4

Minister of Pakistan. How does she feel about such a system? In her own words:

"You go into it without expecting much, and in a certain way this makes the marriage easier. In some cases the chemistry works."

Today, as in olden times, many cultures like to arrange marriages between cousins. Ideally, a Saudi Arabian, Vietnamese or Himalayan girl will marry her mother's brother's son, while a boy weds his father's sister's daughter. This "cross-cousin marriage" is a way of consolidating the family and increasing its power and wealth.

In present-day Japan, a family checking out marriage prospects will sometimes hire a private detective to make sure no embarrassing scandal lurks behind the scenes.

Marriage brokers continue to do a lively business in India, Japan and other countries. They conduct their deals the way job searches are carried out here in America. Armed with detailed resumés and photos of their eligible clients, they visit interested families, giving a sales pitch on behalf of this or that likely young male or female. Usually, the young people meet and must approve of each other before the marriage deal is finalized.

Until very recently, however, oriental brides and grooms did not set eyes on one another until the day of their wedding.

These days, in the Iranian province of Baluchistan, a bride and groom may still not meet until their wedding day. A sign of great progress, however: they now often get to see photographs of one another.

Matchmaking in the U.S. may be relegated to computers and dating services, but in Singapore the government itself has taken the job over. One government agency helps to pair off college graduates, while another one works with those lacking higher education.

In Egypt of the 1990s, parents still do much of the arranging the old-fashioned way. When it's time to get down to business, a young man's mother often phones around asking about good matches for her son. Then, when mother and son go to size up a prospective bride, the girl sits quietly, enveloped in a *galabea* (an ankle-length robe) and veil, with only her face, hands and feet uncovered. If she passes inspection and is chosen, the boy leaves money in a nearby dish.

How does a future mother-in-law examine a cloaked and veiled Egyptian miss? Some women have been known to offer hard nuts to a potential fiancée. If she can crack them with her teeth, at least her choppers are in good shape. Or mama can hug her affectionately to see how she's built and whether she's clean or smelly.

It was much simpler in nineteenth-century Afghanistan. If a man saw a woman he liked, he struck a bargain with her father, cut off a lock of her hair or threw a sheet over her and proclaimed her his bride.

Matchmakers in parts of Russia traditionally loosened their belts before calling on the family of a prospective bride. This supposedly made the girl's parents more receptive to the deal.

In Victorian England, as in America, a suitor took the initiative in the marital wooing—after clearing everything with the girl's father, of course. But here is a forward thinking viewpoint that gives a lady some leeway:

"Under certain circumstances, a woman may go as far as to propose, even when it is not leap-year; a wealthy woman who loves and is loved by a man too proud to propose himself, should not allow two lives to be spoiled by a mistaken sense of honour or false modesty."

–*The Fine Art of Proposing*
by Reverend E. J. Hardy (1909)

In Sudbury, Massachusetts, before marrying, a Puritan girl had to learn candle molding, soap making, weaving, dyeing, broom making and beer brewing. She also had to know how to concoct *mithridate* and *Venice treacle* (antidotes for poison), along with popular household remedies like *palsy drops*, *snail water* or *pokeberry plaster* and a host of other potions and salves.

How do you land your mate? In many cultures people have believed that if your loved one absorbs even a drop of your blood, perspiration or saliva, he or she is yours forever. Just try this old English trick: you prick an orange all over with a needle and sleep with it under your arm. The next day you persuade your beloved to eat it, and you've made a sure conquest.

Or you may prefer the old Ozarks custom of hiding the dried tongue of a turtle dove in your loved one's house...infallible.

When to Tie The Knot

*"Marriage is the clue to human life, but there is
no marriage apart from the wheeling sun and the
nodding earth, from the straying of the planets
and the magnificence of the fixed stars."*

–D.H. Lawrence

The Chinese have traditionally favored the first
new moon of the year or "peach blossom time" for marriages.

Until this century, most New Englanders sched-
uled weddings for March and April (before planting

11

time) or November and December (after harvest). Times to avoid weddings in agricultural communities: May through October (the months of heavy farm work) or the bleak dead of winter.

Many cultures have ruled out May marriages. The superstition "Marry in May and you'll rue it for aye," was popular long before Ovid, who wrote: *Mense malum Maio nubere vulgus ait* ("People say it is bad to wed in the month of May").

Ancient Romans slaughtered a pig and examined the entrails to decide the luckiest time for a couple to wed.

Today, in Muslim, Hindu and Buddhist cultures and in parts of Africa, many families have a priest, monk, astrologer or deviner set an auspicious date for the wedding. This may be done through numerology—based on such things as the couple's names and birth-dates—or the date can be chosen after consulting the stars or the young couple's horoscopes.

Some families have diplomatic reasons for hiring an astrologer before a daughter's wedding. If they decide they don't like a candidate for her hand, they can refuse him and politely blame it on the unlucky stars.

As for the day of the week, this old verse claims to have the answers:

> Monday for wealth,
> Tuesday for health,
> Wednesday best day of all,
> Thursday for losses,
> Friday for crosses,
> And Saturday, no luck at all.

At what age should a person marry? In most developed countries, people tend to wait now until their twenties, after school or college. But early marriages still take place in other societies:

A Bedouin girl of the North Sinai desert may become a bride at age fourteen or fifteen. She will probably begin embroidering her wedding dress at the age of nine, so that the elaborate work will be finished by the time she marries.

Among the Banjara gypsies south of Bombay, an eleven-year-old bride is instructed in customs from the Punjab. She learns to read palms, tell fortunes from cards, sing and dance. She's also taught the precise words to use in addressing her in-laws and her husband, age thirteen.

Here is a custom of early marriage that is no longer observed but was still practiced in the 1960s:

The Shavante Indians of Brazil insisted that all young boys be married off before the older men could take extra wives from the remaining pool. So in a group ceremony, girls of seven or eight were wed to boys of around the same age, chosen by their parents. The brides, all dressed up and frightened out of their wits, were made to lie down beside a row of embarrassed boys with painted faces, while adults performed the marriage rites.

In spite of this traumatic experience, impatient grooms insisted on consummating their marriage—often before the age of ten.

The Case of the Reluctant Bride

"Don't wish me happiness...wish me courage and strength and a sense of humor—I will need them all."

> –Anne Morrow Lindbergh
> (*written just before her marriage*)

Before this century young brides of Asia, Africa, the Middle East, the Philippines and many other regions were expected to put up tremendous resistance when it came time to marry and leave their parents. Like Jewesses of yore, they wailed, writhed and tore their hair in the company of sympathetic girlfriends. Many betrothed maidens even made a show of running away and trying to escape their fate—at least temporarily.

Some historians claim that the reluctant bride is a throwback to a primitive form of marriage: marriage by capture. But in most cases, it was simply good form for a girl to be terribly sensitive about leaving her family and getting deflowered by some big macho brute.

Among the nomads of Central Asia, at wedding time a new bride would gallop off on a horse carrying a newly killed lamb. The groom and his party pursued her until they caught up and seized the lamb, happily ending the escape.

After her wedding, at dusk, an Arab bride ran from tent to tent to avoid going to the tent of her husband. The game was up when, sooner or later, the groom and his friends caught up with her.

Reluctant brides of Wales and Brittany had plenty of help from their friends. When a groom came to get his intended, they would refuse him entrance. When at last they admitted him, he might find the girl disguised as a man, an old lady or a child.

In nineteenth-century China, if a family was slow to produce a promised bride (sometimes due to lack of wedding money rather than the bride's reluctance), often a fiancé had to force the issue. He'd arrive at the girl's house with a bunch of his friends, throw a blanket over her head and cart her off in a sedan chair. Danger: since they probably didn't know what the future bride looked like, sometimes the wrong girl got blanketed!

P.S. — In many cases the reluctant bride syndrome was no pretense at all. A Chinese fiancée, for example, knew she could become the badly mistreated property of her husband. Her moans and tears upon meeting her fate might be most sincere.

❤ ❤ ❤ ❤ ❤ ❤ ❤

These days it's rare to find a bride hiding or screaming in protest at being torn away from her parents. Still, among some people, such as the Bajju of Nigeria, a girl will weep bitter tears en route to her wedding. It would be considered tasteless, *shocking*, if she looked happy about her fate.

A touching rite of separation from the family on the wedding day still endures in some towns and villages. In rural areas of Slovakia, where old-time customs are greatly encouraged, a bride and groom, dressed in traditional garb, stand before their parents and publicly bid them a fond farewell.

Actually, many U.S. marriages now feature a ritual public farewell to dad from the bride. It's the daughter's waltz with her father at the wedding reception. Unspoken but eloquent, the graceful adieu can cause many a dry eye to mist over.

The Village Scene: Invitations and Processions

"To choose a woman for a wife is not to say to Miss So-and-so: You are the ideal of my dreams...To choose a woman for a wife is to say to Miss So-and-so: I want to live with you just as you are...It is you I choose to share my life with me, and that is the only evidence there can be that I love you."

–Denis de Rougemont

In many parts of the world, whole villages may be involved in the wedding festivities. In communist U.S.S.R., the *kolkhoz* (collective farm) often constituted the guest list—and that could be a pretty numerous group. But today, as in times gone by, even larger numbers of villagers may be included in a wedding celebration.

In case you're thinking of the expense, often the village kicks in to help the couple on their way. So why not invite them all?

In the northwestern Greek village of Epirus, two friends or relatives of the bride and groom go from house to house inviting people to the wedding. They bring along a special container of wine and share its contents with all the invited families.

Until recently, in the region of Turkmenistan, paid heralds were sent around the village announcing when and where a wedding would take place. Now, instead, relatives of the couple visit the houses and do their own inviting.

The Meo families of Northern India send emissaries around their village to invite the guests. The emissary offers a small coin (like a penny) to each invitee. If a person accepts the coin, he or she is committed to attend the wedding.

Those invited can look forward to participating in the bridal procession—a major highlight and perhaps the most important feature of the event.

In these parts, we may think of a wedding procession strictly as the bridal party's walk down the aisle and up to the altar. However, in many parts of the world the procession entails large groups of people (in Hungary often the whole village) marching to the bride's home or escorting her to the groom's house or the church.

A bridal procession, as practiced today in the Comoro Islands off the coast of East Africa, is much the same as in ancient Greek times. It's a lively parade with music and dancing in the street. Unlike the Greek way, though, women dance and do a lot of drum beating.

In Russian villages, marchers participating in a wedding procession to the bride's house hand out presents (sweets, fruits, scarves) to people they meet on the way.

A colorful procession takes place these days in the Slovak village of Lendak. There, married women garbed in their local costume carry the bride's possessions, wrapped in bedsheets, to her new home with the groom.

Village weddings, by the way, can be pretty lengthy affairs, lasting at least all day and all night. The Russian ones run about three days and Muslim weddings go on much longer.

Pranks and Pranksters

"Marriage is a three-ring circus. First comes the engagement ring, then the wedding ring—and then the suffer-ring."

–Anonymous

"Strawboys" were once a popular feature at weddings in Ireland. Neighborhood boys would arrive at the wedding reception dressed from head to ankles in costumes of straw. They capered about and generally made mischief until the bridal party offered them presents or food and drink.

Today, in Northern Ireland, prospective brides and grooms are still prey to practical jokes and assorted shenanigans. A soon-to-be-married girl may be seen weirdly dressed, covered with flour, tied to a tree or lamppost, kidnapped by friends, or pushed around in a wheelbarrow.

All over the world, a long tradition of mock battles continues to keep the bride from the groom on their wedding day—at least temporarily:

In the former Yugoslavia, for example, cantankerous villagers block the route of the groom and his party marching to fetch the bride on her wedding day. Usually a gift of some sort must be given to the obstructors before they remove their barrier.

Don't imagine you're safe from this nuisance as far away as Thailand. When a Thai groom arrives at his bride's home, he'll often find the entrance roped-off by members of his own family. He and his party must come across with a few coins in order to get through.

Javanese brides fully expect to be kidnapped by their friends before their wedding. In fact, before marrying, a Javanese girl often has a valise of clothes packed and ready for somebody to send to her place of abduction. (When a girl's parents are strongly opposed to the match, she herself may be party to the kidnapping.)

In the U.S., "bridenapping" (popular in the 1800s) has gone out of fashion along with many other pranks. These days, we rarely see the automobile adorned with streamers, old shoes, rattly cans and conspicuous "Just Married" signs—a familiar sight up until a generation ago. But some mischief does continue...

Here, for example, is a sneaky game sometimes played at American wedding showers:

A friend of the future bride secretly records her comments as she opens each gift. After all have been unwrapped and shown around, the room is silenced and the friend reads her recorded words aloud. They supposedly indicate the bride's reactions on her wedding night—expressions of surprise and joy, exclamations about the size, shape, usefulness or quality of the presents, and so on.

And a less subtle caper: at a Hungarian village wedding reception today, you may see a fun-loving groom and his pals dressed up as brides being merrily chased around by a male sporting a huge artificial penis.

How To Be An African Tribal Bride

"To the nuptial bow'r
I led her blushing like the morn."

—Milton

Well into the twentieth century, many tribal villagers of East and South Africa have kept to their old wedding traditions. Here is how young women of the Rwanda region entered marriage less than a generation ago:

Preliminaries:

On her wedding day, the engaged girl walked to the village hut of her future in-laws enclosed in a large wicker cage that hid all of her but her head and feet. This bulky cage sometimes included a couple of children who accompanied her on her walk.

In some parts of the country, when the bride reached her destination, she stopped outside the door and, before entering, her friends or family would insist on receiving the groom's family cow as a gift.

Frequently, the groom's family presented a little child instead, saying, "Here is the family cow." Sooner or later, however, families that could afford it came across with some sort of livestock. Poor families were known to offer a hoe rather than a cow!

In other regions, the groom greeted the bride by extending his foot and saying, "I give you my *tibia*." (Don't ask why, but somehow this offer of his shinbone really sealed the pact.)

The future mother-in-law frequently greeted the bride by offering her a butter churn and tapping her forehead, chest and shoulders with a spatula. Before she entered the hut, her future father-in-law sprinkled her with a dose of purifying water.

After entering, some brides sat on their future mother-in-law's lap until presented with jewelry or other gifts.

Ceremony and Consummation:

The ceremony began after a crock of homemade beer was passed around to all the guests.

Traditionally, after the groom placed a wreath of ivy (*umwishywa*) on the bride's head, he would spit a ritual liquid (*imbazi*) in her face. This wreathing and spitting were, until recently, the main ingredients of the ceremony.

These days, however, modern natives of Rwanda prefer the words "I take you as my wife" to spitting *imbazi* at the girl.

The conjugal act is referred to as "getting *umwishywa*," which literally means "receiving the wedding ivy wreath." In the past, before a married couple could have their *umwishywa*, the groom's parents had to retire to their room and accomplish the act themselves.

The following night, when the bride and groom were to consummate their marriage, a younger brother of the bride would slip between the two until the groom convinced him to leave.

The bride was expected to put up a fierce resistance to losing her virginity, until duty or passion conquered all.

Rings and Things

"It is commonly a weak man who marries for love."

—Samuel Johnson

"Love is not a weakness. It is strong. Only the sacrament of marriage can contain it."

—Boris Pasternak

For centuries, engagement and wedding rings have graced the second finger of the left hand. Why? Because people such as the ancient Egyptians believed a vein ran directly from that finger to the heart.

Still, some cultures have favored other digits. Before the seventeenth century, English women wore

33

the ring on their right hand and brides of ancient Rome sported it on their thumb.

A twentieth-century Greek betrothal is a double ring ceremony, in which the rings are placed on the second finger of the right hand and exchanged three times.

The earliest betrothal rings were made of braided grass, rushes or hemp. Then they appeared in more durable materials, such as leather and stone as time went on, and iron for the early Romans.

Gold rings were used as currency before coins in ancient Egypt. An Egyptian wealthy enough to afford it might give his bride a gold ring to show that he entrusted her with his property.

In Italy, gold and the imperishable diamond for betrothal rings came into vogue among the wealthy gentry during the middle ages.

Centuries ago, grooms presented rings as partial payment for the bride.

Our Puritan fathers frowned on wedding rings, deeming them "frivolous jewelry" or, as one religious spoilsport put it, "a relic of Popery."

Later, in colonial times, someone started the custom of giving an engaged girl a "wedding thimble." After the marriage, the bottom cup of the thimble was cut off and—*voila!*—the top part became a wedding ring.

Here Comes the Bride All Dressed in...?

"I...chose my wife, as she did her wedding gown, not for a fine glossy surface but such qualities as would wear well."

–Oliver Goldsmith

"I personally adore marriage...I even cry at weddings, especially my own."

–Zsa Zsa Gabor

Chances are you'll say "white." However, that virginal color didn't really catch on before the mid-nineteenth century. Before that, brides simply put on their best dress or the traditional wedding costume of their country, whatever the color.

37

Some say the white wedding dress came into fashion when some upper-class misses decided to show off their wealth, preferring one-time white to dark-hued dresses that could be worn over and over again.

Customary colors for brides:

> black in Spain;
> red in China and Islamic cultures;
> white in Japan;
> blue in Russia.

Blue, long considered a symbol of purity, has been favored on wedding days. In ancient times, Hebrew brides wore blue ribbons on their wedding garments as proof of their virginity.

Most societies have frowned on yellow for wedding dresses: people have seen that color as a sure sign of a wife's intention to cheat on her husband.

That is not the case in Korea, where brides today still wear fabulous ceremonial robes of bright reds and yellows on their wedding day.

> "Married in white, you have chosen all right;
> Married in grey, you will go far away;
> Married in black, you will wish yourself back;
> Married in red, you will wish yourself dead;
> Married in green, ashamed to be seen;
> Married in pearl, you will live in a whirl;
> Married in yellow, ashamed of your fellow;
> Married in brown, you will live out of town;
> Married in pink, your fortune will sink."

–Old Victorian verse

Brides have worn veils since ancient Greek and Roman times. In some cultures, the veil was thought to protect a bride from evil spirits.

Muslim countries keep their women veiled throughout their adult lives (the custom of *purdah* in India), to hide their charms from men's leering glances.

Early Roman veils were the color of flame.

In Muslim and Shinto societies, veils have traditionally covered the bride's head completely. Often an Asian groom's first glimpse of his wife was upon lifting her veil on their wedding day.

A bride of colonial America wore no veil at all.

A Shower of Flowers

> "The kind of love which will enable a marriage to remain happy and to fulfil its social purpose is not romantic but is something more intimate, affectionate and realistic."
>
> –Bertrand Russell

A 1907 Victorian manual on "good style and deportment" had the following advice for a suitor courting an eligible female:

The young man could send her pansies, meaning: "I'm thinking of you," along with a moss rosebud telling her: "I now confess my love." If the lady sends him back wild daisies, that signifies: "I'll think about it." Garden daisies will let him know she truly shares his tender feelings.

If by chance she rejects him, he may send her purple hyacinths (*slighted love*), yellow crysanthemums (*separation*) and jasmine (*sorrow*). Then, to show kindness in this "war of the posies," the maid can offer him a consolation prize of platonic love—a spray of rose acacia. Or she may even change her mind and get him back again with a gift of silver leaf geranium.

Today, some American shower parties include the old English custom of the shower bouquet. Originally, these consisted of ribbons and roses, tied together, with the ribbons cut in varying lengths. Nowadays, a friend of the bride may use colorful ribbons from the shower gifts and paper plates from the party. As each package is opened, she fits the ends of ribbons through slits in a paper plate, keeping the graceful bows on top and letting the long ends trail underneath.

Throwing the bridal bouquet, like throwing the garter, apparently came from the age-old English custom of "flinging the stocking":

On the wedding night, guests invaded the couple's chamber. There, a girl would seize the groom's stocking and throw it backwards over her head from the foot of the bed, trying to whop the groom with it. The girl who hit her mark would marry within a year. (The same applied to any man who managed to score a bull's eye on the bride with her own stocking.)

Some flowers for a wedding bouquet and what they symbolize:

> Orange blossoms for happiness and fertility;
> Red roses for love;
> Red and white roses combined for unity;
> White lilac for innocence;
> Lily of the valley for purity;
> Orchids for beauty;

Ivy for fidelity;
Rosemary for remembrance;
Sage for domestic virtue;
Marigolds for sensual passion.

The Bond of Food and Drink

"…a man likes a wife to be fat and plump, for he then experiences, when he sleeps with her, a pleasure which he does not have with a thin woman."

—Arab Book of Marriage, 11th century

The word "bridal" originated from the old English *bridale*, a combination of "bride" and "ale" that came to mean "wedding feast."

In early America, a Puritan girl and boy who ate from the same trencher (wooden plate) were considered engaged.

The Japanese bride and groom celebrate their bond by drinking *sake* together.

The Jewish wedding couple commemorates it by sipping from the same cup of consecrated wine.

A Javanese bride and groom feed each other three times from a plate of rice.

A Muslim couple bites into the same piece of candy.

Today in America, newlyweds who feed each other with the first slice of wedding cake hark back to Ancient Rome, when couples pledged their troth by sharing food.

Those Good Luck Charms

"Marriage is a lottery in which men stake their
liberty and women their happiness."

–Madame de Rieux

"Something old; something new;
Something borrowed; something blue."

Something old: a bride wears some old or used
object the day of her wedding as a symbol of continuity
with the past.

Something new: that represents an optimistic
token, a charm for a sunny future in the marriage.

Something borrowed: she should borrow some little thing from a happily married friend or relative, since married bliss is said to rub off on others.

Something blue: because blue symbolizes purity, fidelity and love.

Many a Greek bride believes a lump of sugar, tucked into her wedding glove, will bring her sweetness throughout her married life.

Uzbek-Durmen women of Russia have been known to keep their wedding dresses unhemmed, to ensure good luck in marriage.

At Benazir Bhutto's 1987 wedding, her mother and aunts ground sugar cones over the couple, then knocked their heads together for a solid union.

In some cultures, friends tie the wedding couple's clothes together for unity. Ribbon bows have been traditional wedding favors, symbolizing the marriage knot.

Superstition has it that when the bride cuts the first piece of wedding cake, she'll be sure to have children. Some couples save a piece of cake to eat on their first anniversary, for luck and a long life together.

The Irish peasantry used to take a hen about to lay an egg and tie it to the bridal bed on the wedding night to ensure fertility.

After a Thai wedding, the bride and groom each hold the palms of their hands together in a praying position. Then guests pour water through the palms, wishing them fertility and good luck in their wedded life.

As in the past, a Korean groom today will ask a happily married friend to fashion two small wooden ducks for his new household, since ducks mate for life.

Designs of cranes, also symbols of life-long fidelity, are often sewn into traditional oriental wedding robes.

In India, besides decorating the bride's hands with henna (for protection against evil), turmeric is rubbed on both bride and bridegroom to ensure their happiness.

In present-day Egypt, women like to pinch a bride—it supposedly brings good luck.

$\mathcal{A}$ Seven-Day Muslim Wedding

"Marriage, if one will face the truth, is an evil,
but a necessary evil."

–Menander

"Marriage is a wonderful institution; but then
again, so is a bicycle repair kit."

–Billy Connolly

The traditional week-long Muslim wedding can
get very expensive these days, especially in the big cities;
but people are still having them in Egypt, Lebanon,
Morocco and other Islamic countries. This is how they
do it in Morocco:

Day #1: The bride is beautified. A hired professional woman arrives at her house with precious old dynasty jewels rented for the occasion and an ample supply of henna. The bride, wearing traditional Morrocan garb, has her hair dressed by the woman.

The visiting woman removes unwanted hair from the girl. In a Bedouin village all the bride's body hair is shaved off, in accordance with an ancient custom dating from the pharaohs. But in more sophisticated regions, her pubic hair is usually spared and the rest removed with wax depilatory.

Here is a depilatory recipe used for brides in present-day Egypt:

- 2 1/2 C sugar
- 2 C water
- the juice of one lemon

Bring the mixture to a boil and simmer for 20–30 minutes, or until it becomes a thick paste (don't let it burn). Cool it slightly. Spread the mixture on the bride's arms and legs. Let it stand for a half hour, then remove it. The bride's skin will be smooth and will smell nicely.

The professional then peforms her artistry, drawing lacy "gloves" on the girl's hands and "stockings" on her feet with a needle filled with henna. (The henna decorations last for days unless scoured off.)

Day #2: For females only. At a lavish buffet, featuring lots of sweets, the women eat, gossip and dance to the strains of an orchestra hired for the occasion.

Day #3: The men have their day, while the women folk stay out of sight in quarters nearby.

Day #4: The sheik, a Muslim priest, arrives and unites the pair. Usually, in Muslim countries, only females are invited to the wedding ceremony.

Days #5 and #6: General fiesta. Invited relatives and friends enjoy the festivities, which include food, Arab and Andalusian music and bellydancing performances.

Day #7: The bride is carried in the air. As in many other cultures, the Moroccan bride is considered a queen. She is dressed most elegantly, in a special dress decorated with pearls and gold, and she wears a sphinx-shaped headdress. Now she is lifted high up and carried about like a royal figure.

Who does the carrying? The very same woman who supplies the henna painting and the rented jewels (a bargain, this package deal). Since bride-lifting is part of how she earns a living, her muscles make an impressive sight as she circles the room, holding her cargo high for at least two hours.

The bride finally comes down to earth and into the arms of her groom.

Lest anyone get bored by this uplifting experience, there are, as usual, plenty of munchies around. In fact, in wealthy households servants begin cooking for the big event one month in advance. Small wonder the most recent trend is to shorten the festivities to three days total.

Rice and Confetti for Fertility

*"Lover—husband—wife—mother—father—
child—home!—without these sacred words the
world is but a lair, and men and women merely
beasts."*

–Matthew Arnold

Nearly all cultures have showered the wedding couple with symbolic food to grant them a large harvest of babies.

The French have traditionally thrown wheat at the bridal couple and Sicilians wheat bread and salt, while the English have used pieces of cake.

In some parts of England, rather than tossing bits of cake at the couple, bridal guests ensured their fertility by smashing a plate of salt over the groom's head.

Early Romans threw nuts and seeds, and Greeks liked to fling nuts, dates and seed-bearing plants. (Today, the Greek favor dates, almond candies and rice.)

Bulgarians, somewhat heavier of hand, have hurled figs.

Modern Americans—even those concerned with the world's overpopulation—throw rice. Someone who may have considered that sport too dangerous (or wasteful) came up with the idea of substituting delicate paper confetti. That's just fine with modern environmentalists, who warn that rice may harm birds, being hard for them to digest.

Bridesmaids, Thresholds and Things That Go Bump in the Night

"Never let your husband see your sleeping face."

–Old Japanese saying

"Never marry a widow unless her first husband was hanged."

–Old English Proverb

From earliest times, societies have surrounded the bride and groom with superstitions. Families and friends of the newlyweds have been especially on guard against evil spirits threatening the couple's happiness.

After all, a jilted lover might put a jealous hex on the marriage, leaving the wife sexually unsatisfied and barren. And then there are always those nasty invisible demons lurking in the background, eager to spoil things out of pure spite.

Not to worry. People have devised a million ways of foiling the enemy and ridding the wedding day of "ghosties and ghoulies and long-legged beasties and things that go bump in the night..."

♥ ♥ ♥ ♥ ♥ ♥ ♥

Why are bridesmaids dressed alike? Why do the best man and ushers look like clones of the groom? In primitive times, the wedding couple were surrounded by friends of the same age group, all dressed similarly, so that the evil spirits might not zero in on the real bride and groom.

In old Denmark, wedding couples used to wear clothes of the opposite sex, to confuse the demons.

In India, to protect the couple, as part of the wedding ceremony each was symbolically married to a tree.

Today, when brides of Lebanon, India, Egypt and other Muslim and African countries are painted with henna, it is because henna leaf dye supposedly makes them unrecognizable to the evil eye.

Watch out for knots! A Syrian groom must make sure no enemy has placed a knotted object among his clothes. If he winds up wearing a knot at the ceremony, impotence could be his fate.

The threshold to a bride's new home can be a dangerous place. After all, who knows what horrible magic lies there? Clever (and muscular) bridegrooms still avoid trouble by carrying their spouses across in their arms.

A bride of ancient Rome rubbed the doorpost of her new home with grease to erase any evil. She also got carried over the threshold because it was believed that if she stumbled walking in, harm could befall the marriage.

In the past, Armenians and Arabians sacrificed sheep at the wedding couple's threshold. The newlyweds stepped over the blood and were henceforth protected.

A modern Egyptian groom carries his bride from the automobile across the threshold. Water is splashed over the doorway area to clear away any magic put there by jealous spirits.

The honking of horns in a modern wedding motorcade harks back to the noisy traditions of clanging bells and shooting guns to frighten away evil spirits.

The Virgin Bride

"I should say that the majority of women (happily for them) are not very much troubled with sexual feeling of any kind...The best mothers, wives, and managers of households know little or nothing of sexual indulgences. Love of home, children, and domestic duties are the only passions they feel."

–William Acton (1857)

According to *Deuteronomy*, if any man takes a wife and discovers she's not a virgin, "the men of her city shall stone her with stones that she die."

Puritan New England shared those same sentiments. In 1638, John Bickerstaffe and Ales Burwoode, like a number of other courting couples, received severe whip lashings. He got them for "enticing her"—she "for not crying out."

The ideal of virginity continues strong today in Muslim and Hindu cultures. An Indonesian girl who runs away with her suitor despite her parents' opposition will probably wind up marrying him. This is because—even if she hasn't consummated the affair—she will now be considered "damaged goods" and unfit to marry anyone else.

In present-day Saudi Arabia—as in parts of Iran and Pakistan—a girl who loses her virginity before marrying may be punished, even murdered, along with her lover, by outraged males of her own family.

But...other countries, other mores. Tahiti has long had the reputation of being a sexual paradise. Here is Diderot's account of what the explorer Bougainville and his men must have experienced when they sailed to that tropical isle. In this story a Tahiti native, Orou, invites Bougainville's Catholic chaplain to spend the night with a female of his family:

"If you sleep alone you'll sleep poorly. A man needs a lady companion at his side. There are my wife and my daughters. Choose any one of them, but if you want to oblige me you'll take my youngest daughter who hasn't had any children yet."

After many protests ("But my religion!"), the chaplain finally gives in, and the next morning the couple is greeted by happy family members surrounding their bed and congratulating them for conceivably conceiving a future member of the Tahiti community.

Tahiti was not an isolated case. Men of eastern Tibet traditionally lent their wives and daughters to strangers, in order to obtain the favor of the gods.

Among the tribes of central Australia, before a husband took pleasure with his bride, the breaking of her hymen was the business of another male tribal member. Who had first priority? Her maternal grandfather, believe it or not. If he wasn't alive, willing or able, the task fell to a cousin on her mother's side.

Eskimos brought their brides to a priest for a divine deflowering.

During the middle ages in Europe, and even later, the lord of the manor had the legal right to spend the first night with any non-noble bride on his land (*"le droit du seigneur"*).

Heroditus recorded that the women of the ancient Gindanes wore leather bands around their ankles for each man who made love to them, and "she who has the most bands is the most esteemed," since she has been loved by the greatest number of men.

How to Recognize a Jewish Wedding

"One advantage of marriage, it seems to me, is that when you fall out of love with him, or he falls out of love with you, it keeps you together until you maybe fall in again."

–Judith Viorst

The modern Jewish wedding doesn't differ radically from a Christian one, but it has a number of important symbols and traditions that clearly set it apart.

There is first of all the *ketubah*, the Hebrew marriage contract dating from the end of the first century and still in use today. Much like the ancient Egyptian contract, the *ketubah* was designed mainly to assure the bride's legal status and protect her rights. But that contract, often just a formality these days, is not a conspicuous feature of most marriage ceremonies.

If we actually attend a Jewish wedding—whether at the home of a blue collar worker or at a posh Park Avenue temple—we are immediately aware of some very visible symbols that mark the wedding as a Jewish one.

Of course there are the *yamulkes*, those little beanie caps (usually white for weddings) worn by the rabbi, the groom, the wedding party and male guests.

Then, instead of an altar you will see a *huppah*, an improvised canopy attached to four poles, under which the couple will be wed. (The origin of that custom is now lost, but other Middle Eastern civilizations have used bamboo posts topped with boughs and leaves at their weddings.)

The procession down the aisle is different, too. In most Christian marriages, the father of the bride walks to the altar to give his daughter away, while the other parents sit teary-eyed in their pews. At a Jewish wedding, usually both parents of the bride and groom will escort their children to the *huppah*, demonstrating involvement of the whole family.

And there is that exotic tradition: the breaking of the glass. After the ceremony has been recited in Hebrew and English, the groom stomps on a glass (wrapped in cloth in order not to bloody anyone) as people applaud or shout "*mazeltov*" (congratulations).

The broken glass symbol has many interpretations. For some, it signifies the frailty of human happiness; for others, it refers to the destruction of the Israelite Temple in the year 70 A.D. In the past, some Jewish husbands have insisted that it means *they* will have all the authority in the household. (Who would dare say that these days?) But one of the oldest and most common interpretations of broken glass at weddings is the easing of sexual penetration on the first night of marriage.

(Sicily, Greece and England, among other countries, have also had the custom of breaking glass at weddings. In the Greek village of Epirus today, when the bride leaves her house, she kicks a glass of wine placed at her doorstep. If it breaks, the marriage will be successful.)

The festivities at a Jewish wedding reception will nearly always include, besides ballroom dancing, a round of that lively Israeli circle dance, the *hora*. At times, it may be accompanied by a real old-world *klezmer* band, combining Eastern European Jewish themes and traces of modern jazz.

Next comes the grand finale. As in other cultures, the Jewish bride and groom are considered royalty, at least for a day. So they are each enthroned and their chairs are lifted high in the air over the dancing, cheering guests.

When couples are aloft, you will usually see them each clutching one end of a handkerchief or cloth napkin. This symbolizes their union, but it also reminds us that in former times Jewish couples, even married ones, were not allowed to touch each other in public.

Sometimes, in their enthusiasm, the bridal party will also hoist up the chairs containing the couple's parents. That can get a bit hairy, however, especially if mom and dad are unaccustomed to levitation outside a 747.

Now, traditionally, one of a Jewish mother's main goals in life was to marry off all her children. That—besides being a perfect housekeeper—was a sure sign of her success. So if by chance the bride or groom is the last child to be married off, you may see and participate in the joyful *krentsl* dance.

The mother of the last marriageable child is crowned with a wreath of leaves, a *krentsl* (a Yiddish diminutive of *kranz*, the German word for "wreath").

Then, family and friends surround the lucky lady and joyfully dance around her.

Meanwhile, a sumptuous meal, sometimes lasting hours, will bring the event to its conclusion.

So, if you knew nothing about Jewish weddings before reading this, now you can say when you go to one, "By jove, this is a Jewish wedding!"

More Enduring Superstitions

"The men that women marry, and why they marry them will always be a mystery to the world."

—Henry Wadsworth Longfellow

"No woman should marry a teetotaller…"

—Robert Louis Stevenson

Many natives of Bali are convinced, even today, that a magician or guru can make you fall in love and marry the wrong person, through a magic spell called *guna-guna*.

The Dolgan people of Siberia believe it a great sin to remain single, for after death the soul of a bachelor becomes *dzheretinnik* (heretic). Instead of resting in the land of the dead, it stays on earth to frighten the living.

In the Tobelo village of eastern Indonesia, a bride must not see her image in a mirror when she is decorated for the wedding—her face adorned with white dots and her breasts with ancestral coins. In fact, she and her husband should also avoid seeing photos of her so decorated, for as long as twenty years afterwards.

What's in a name? The Bantu of Tanzania consider it shameful to address a spouse by his or her real name. Instead, they will use the father's name. (For example, a man will call his wife "Daughter of Masanja.")

Among the Bantu and people of other African tribes, a wife should never speak with her father-in-law, nor a husband with his mother-in-law. A wife disappears immediately if she notices her father-in-law approaching the house. Outside, a man gives his mother-in-law wide berth if he spots her coming his way.

Then there is that very enduring Indian superstitious custom of *suttee*. Do you remember Shirley MacLaine in *Around the World in 80 Days*? As a widow in India, she was supposed to be burned alive, along with her dead husband (she happily escaped her fate, thanks to David Niven, who played Phineas Fogg). Although no ancient Muslim law sanctions *suttee*, and in spite of modern legislation prohibiting it, many in India still believe it to be a holy practice.

Several widows committed *suttee* throughout the 1980s. Some were poor and perhaps desperate; others were pushed into it by the groom's family. In 1987, a beautiful, well-educated Indian woman of twenty-three, married scarcely six months, was immolated alive on her husband's funeral pyre before a mass of three thousand cheering spectators.

Money Matters (Does it Ever!)

"It is a truth universally acknowledged that a single man in possession of a good fortune, must be in want of a wife."

–Jane Austen

In Japan of the 1990s, the average cost of a wedding equals $28,554. That includes, among other things: the Shinto wedding ceremony; a wedding hall reception for 100 guests—with banquet, master of ceremonies, karaoke, videotaping, flowers and music; around four changes of clothes for the bride (often two kimonos, a western-style white gown and a going-away suit); the groom's formal attire; gifts for the guests and the honeymoon.

At a Japanese wedding reception, guests line up to hand the bride envelopes full of cash (usually the equivalent of $150-$200 per person). The gifts they themselves receive from the bride and groom may be of greater value than their cash contributions.

When a wedding couple is considered really important, guests usually up the ante. A few years ago, a niece of ex-emperor Hirohito married a descendant of a great tea master. They received in the neighborhood of $140 million in cash and gifts.

In Pakistan, the traditional red-and-gold bridal robe alone can cost the equivalent of $450 to $9,000, or several months' income for the average Pakistani household.

For Saudi Arabians, wedding expenses, covered mainly by the bride's side, can eat up the net worth of her family. They usually go the whole route, however, since their honor is at stake.

For economy-minded brides and grooms, some hotels and wedding palaces in Singapore and Tokyo now offer a package deal when ten or twenty couples marry at the same time. To make the multiple marriage ceremony even more attractive, often a honeymoon trip is thrown in.

The ancient custom of the dowry still exists in many countries. Most often, however, the heftiest contributions come not from the bride but from the groom as a "brideprice"—an offering by the man's family in exchange for his wife. Today, this often consists of cash or gold jewelry (although in some places, it's still cows or pigs).

Males in the Koguru tribe of Tanzania customarily pay a brideprice in return for a promise of marriage.

These days they do it in cash, but they hand the money over in segments named after the objects they used to contribute in the past. A certain sum will be referred to as a female goat, another as the chain necklace traditionally given to the bride's father, and so on.

"Wed" comes from an old English word meaning pledge: a man pledges goods or property in exchange for the bride. (By the way, did you know "wages" came from the same word?)

Many fathers have sold their daughters to the highest bidder—even if she cared not a whit for him. Today, that's less common than it used to be and usually illegal. However, it still happens in China, in poor areas of Pakistan, India and elsewhere.

Here is one 1993 case of a "bartered bride" in the Dani community of Irian Jaya: In exchange for the hand of his twelve-year-old daugher, a father demanded twenty pigs from the groom (he actually settled for eleven).

Getting the highest brideprice from a suitor is, of course, a major concern. But how far will a girl go to strike the best deal? Here's one example:

These days, Surma women of Ethiopia continue to stretch their lower lips with plates in order to get a substantial brideprice for their parents. Evidently the farther an enticing lip protrudes, the more a groom will pay. Recently, one very large-lipped woman secured a windfall of over fifty cattle.

In case the idea appeals to you, this is how it's done: a small hole is painfully pierced in a Surma girl's lower lip when she is around age 20. A tiny disk is inserted in it, then larger and larger plates are substituted until the skin of the lip is remarkably stretched. (Women do remove the plates, however, to eat and chat with each other.)

Women of Ethiopia's Mursi tribe begin the jutting lower lip process earlier, at the first signs of puberty.

Two lower teeth are extracted before an incision is made in the lower lip and a wooden plug inserted in it. Again, the "wannabe brides" wear disks of increasing size in their quest for beauty and a high brideprice.

In the past, since the Turkmen workers of Central Asia could rarely pay the full brideprice up front, after the wedding the bride would go home to live with her parents—sometimes for ten to fifteen years—until he could come up with the whole amount.

Still, that's not quite as bad as the case of Jacob in the Old Testament. He agreed to work seven years for Rachel's father before he could marry her. Then—surprise!—after his seven years of "brideservice" were up, his future father-in-law handed him Rachel's older sister, Leah. So poor Jacob had to labor another seven years to get Rachel, too.

Today, a Murle groom of Southern Sudan must pay as much as forty head of cattle as his brideprice.

Because this bovine fortune takes so long to amass, bachelors there must delay marrying. So meanwhile, to be assured a stake in the wife market, they keep a sharp eye on young flirtatious boys and don't even allow them to hold dances of their own. Any young males who get too frisky with girls their age may be beaten with sticks by their elders.

Among the Mayan T'oj Nam of Guatemala, the groom's cash payment to a bride's family increased 700% over the past thirty-five years—at the same rate of inflation as the regional staple, corn.

In Sri Lanka, a middle class groom's payment to the bride's family runs around $10,000, and he hands it over publicly on his wedding day. With women in the minority, however, it's often the bride who kicks in with a cash dowry—behind the scenes, that is.

In many societies, families regularly save money to cover these wedding expenses the way contemporary Americans do to cover their children's college education.

As for a girl's dowry, some parents in Latin America, the Middle and Far East (like Frenchwomen before World War I) begin putting money aside as soon as a daughter is born.

Dowries were set up mainly to help a man ease the financial burden incurred by taking on a wife. European dowries commonly used to feature land or a daughter's share in property owned by her family.

Today, dowries frequently come in the shape of useful goods. A modern Japanese bride, for example, may enter marriage with complete furnishings for a new home.

In large cities of South America or the Middle East, a well-heeled bride's dowry might include, besides jewelry, a fridge, a VCR or an air conditioner.

Yams are often dowry in Papua, New Guinea. There, women have complete control over the yam harvest, and their produce may substantially enrich a marriage.

As antiquated as the dowry system may appear to us, it can protect a married woman. Her dowry usually reverts to her if she becomes widowed or divorced. On the other hand (in most cases these days), if the marriage fails, the groom cannot get back the bridewealth he contributed. That stays with the wife's family.

And the higher the brideprice he pays, the less apt he is to break up the marriage, knowing he'll never see his money or his cows again.

Our present-day American bridal shower is a traditional way of replacing or adding to the dowry or brideprice.

How did the custom start? According to an old legend, a young maiden of Holland loved a miller's son, but her father couldn't afford the huge dowry demanded by the boy's father. So all the people of the village chipped in and "showered" gifts on the couple, enabling them to set up housekeeping.

Dancing with the bride can help too. In some villages of Hungary and Spain today, as in the past, men make a cash contribution to the new wife each time they whirl her around the floor.

Some areas of Korea now have a new custom of bridal "Kowtow money." At wedding time, the bride sinks to her knees and makes profound, complicated bows before her relatives and future in-laws, whereupon they leave cash contributions on a handy tray.

♥ ♥ ♥ ♥ ♥ ♥ ♥ ♥

Now, if all the expense and rigamarole of a wedding sound too overwhelming to you, perhaps you would prefer to follow a custom of Pagatepan, a village in the north of Bali. There, fathers hate to see their daughters take a husband. Not only because a legal marriage in Pagatepan costs a lot and entails red tape galore, but because they want to keep their girls as a precious source of labor. For these and other reasons, parents often don't even show up at a daughter's wedding.

So, this is how nearly half the marriages take place there these days.

How to Elope in Pagatepan

"It is better to marry than to burn."

–Paul the Apostle

1. An eloping girl waits for her suitor at a pre-arranged out-of-the-way spot, her suitcase packed with clothes.

2. The would-be groom comes to get her with an abducting party of three or more members, including at least one female to reassure the runaway girl, and at least one member of the boy's family, to show his kin's support.

3. They whisk the girl away to the home of a respectable older couple (ideally the suitor's grandparents), where she is given temporary lodging. Meanwhile, the boy hides out in another place.

4. Once the runaway couple are safely out of sight, a member of the abducting party goes up to the girl's house, shouts the news of the elopement, and speeds away in order not to be caught and beaten by the girl's angry family.

5. Now it is fix-it time. First, a respected family or community member is asked by the boy to visit the girl's parents and try to work out some sort of settlement. Then it is important to enlist the support of the religious community, so spokesmen (or better still, spokeswomen) for the girl go to the village's religious scholars and apologize for her discourteous behavior.

6. If the father consents to the marriage, so much the better. But if not, a legal marriage takes place without his approval. The elders of the village appoint a representative to replace the father and to iron out details of the groom's brideprice contribution.

7. A simple ceremony follows, including a meal of rice and meat, with the officiating priest (the *imam*) taking the major portion home in a "doggie bag" made of banana leaves.

8. Some days after consummating their marriage, the couple makes "begging pardon" calls (called *ngunya*) on the bride's family members. The food they bring on these apologetic visits has both a spiritual and a sensual meaning:

The *bantal*—long, thin sweets tightly tied with purple string—symbolize an unbreakable marriage bond. They also refer to the string of the traditional *sarong*, untied by the husband on the wedding night.

The *pasung*—flattened packages of white and sweetish-brown rice meal wrapped in leaves—symbolize keeping the heart sweet. The sensual meaning: white semen and a brown female secretion, for a sweet, successful sexual intercourse.

The *cerorot*—phallic shaped cones of pudding wrapped in a coconut leaf spiral—are eaten by unwrapping the leaf and squeezing out the pudding. Spiritual significance: happiness with one wife. Sexual meaning: pretty obvious.

❤ ❤ ❤ ❤ ❤ ❤ ❤

Elopement in Pagatepan may sound a bit complicated, but it seems to be working for the Pagatepanis.

(Among the Porja tribe of North India and the African Shona people, what people call "marriage by capture" there is really a staged abduction, another type of elopement by mutual consent. In those places, however, the elopement system is a thousand times simpler than in Pagatepan.)

The Wedding Night

....or...

Alone at Last

"A successful marriage requires falling in love
many times, always with the same person."
—Mignon McLaughlin

As a matter of fact, traditionally, brides and
grooms were rarely left alone on their wedding night. In
nineteenth-century America, as in Europe and the East,
the wedding chamber seemed a great place to continue
the party.

Often a horde of villagers crowded in, drinking up a storm, singing bawdy songs, flinging stockings at the bride's and groom's noses and generally making mischief, as the luckless couple lay abed, wondering when the mob would finally clear out.

Worse than that, in some places it was customary for the bridal party to hang around and witness the consummation.

Speaking of uninvited guests, here's a custom still seen in the 1990s in some parts of Africa and the Orient: The bride's family will place a little child—perhaps the bride's younger brother—in bed with the couple. That supposedly ensures fertility, but kicking out a sleeping (or obstinate) kid can sometimes be a tough proposition.

The bride and groom finally fulfill their mission and consummate the marriage. But wait—the fuss isn't over yet. Today, in many Muslim communities and parts of Greece, the groom is still expected to display virginal blood on the sheets the morning after.

In Crete and Sparta, the groom appears at their window in the morning. When friends waiting outside are assured the bride was a virgin before marriage, they shoot guns off in order to announce the happy news to the whole village.

What if the unthinkable happens and the bride was too obliging—or impatient—to keep intact until her wedding? Some thoughtful friends might kill a chicken and collect the blood for the groom to smear on the sheet.

Unfortunately, many a village matron, even without DNA, is sure she can tell the difference between blood of chicken and blood of virgin girl.

In olden times, some grooms tried to give their brides back the morning after, claiming they were definitely not chaste maidens before they wed. According to *Deuteronomy*, in such cases the bride's parents could take the marriage bedding (stained hopefully with blood of maiden) and spread it before the elders. If they prevailed, the groom might be punished.

As for the bride, she was minus one husband but at least she had her reputation.

Returning to present-day newlyweds, once they have overcome any hurdles of the first night and morning after, they may find life fairly easy—at least for one week. In Egypt, as in certain other countries, the bride's family does all the cooking for seven days so the couple can relax. In some villages, this family food service can go on for a whole month.

The Married Couple:
Their Conduct and Duties

"A successful marriage is an edifice that must be
rebuilt every day."

–Andre Maurois

"Marriage…is a damnably serious business, particularly around Boston."

–John Phillips Marquand

Proper etiquette for married couples in the early twentieth century:

When newlyweds returned from their honeymoon, their wedding guests and friends had to call at their house immediately or, in their absence, leave a visiting card. Said friends were also supposed to visit the bride's mother within two or three weeks after the wedding.

Every model wife understood that gentlemen, including her husband, always offered her their right arm, unless they were descending a staircase, in which case she would have the wall side, for safety.

Another rule: "A husband and wife never enter a ballroom arm in arm."

Puritan America had its own regulations, and one was: no hanky-panky permitted in public between married couples. A certain Captain Kemble had that drummed into him when he returned home to Charlestown, Massachusetts after a long, three-year voyage. He eagerly greeted his wife in front of their house and impulsively kissed her right there, in full view of the neighbors. The court sentenced him to two hours in the stocks for "lewd and unseemly behavior."

Kissing your mate in public was unthinkable even in the permissive upper-class society of eighteenth-century France. In fact in that milieu, no self-respecting lady would be seen around town with her own husband. And few of them would admit to actually being in love with him—that would be too *bourgeois*.

But let us consider more practical domestic matters—meals, for example:

In England and continental Europe, wives or female servants carved the meat until the mid-nineteenth century, when the job fell to husbands and male servants.

Well into this century, in a French peasant household, a wife served meals to her husband and any other male diners, while she herself ate standing up.

The time-honored custom of excluding women from the male meal continues today in Muslim countries, where married females still organize their own, carefully choreographed, hen parties.

And these days in Java at the *slametan*—a meal served on important occasions—women do the cooking, but are not allowed to eat with the men.

Figi cannibals customarily reserved human flesh for males of their tribe. It was considered too good to be wasted on the women.

At the present time, Japanese girls can prepare for marriage in places like Ikenobo College, Kyoto, learning such duties as flower arranging, performing tea ceremonies and managing a household.

In nineteenth-century America, some wives of plantation owners worked nearly as hard around the house as their female slaves. Martha Forman, married in 1814 to General Forman, a wealthy Maryland plantation owner, was on her feet from 4:00 a.m. to 11:00 p.m.

almost every day. Among her daily activities were the following:

Making thirty to thirty-four pounds of old tallow into candles; cutting out fourteen shirts, jackets or trousers for the slaves (whom she always called "the people" or "our family"); knitting stockings; washing, dyeing and spinning wool; baking mince pies and potato puddings; sewing wheat or reaping it; killing farm animals and salting the meat; planting or picking fruits and vegetables; making jams, jellies and preserves with her fruit; helping whitewash or paint walls; ironing; preparing for large parties; caring for sick family and slaves.

Speaking of working wives, this turn-of-the-century newspaper quotation from an American farmer says it all:

"Is marriage a success? I should say so. Why, there's my Hetty, gits up in the a.m., milks six cows, gits breakfast, starts four children to school, looks after the other three, feeds the hens, likewise the pigs, and some orphin lambs, skims twenty pans of milk, washes the cloes, cooks the dinner, et cetery, et cetery. Think I could hire anybody to do it for what she gits? Not much. Marriage is a success, sir, a very great success. I've tried both and I know."

Advice for Sexy Singles and Wedded Women

"A man *always* objects if you do something drastic to yourself like changing your hair color or losing fifteen pounds or wearing a miniskirt, even though he kept telling you at yesterday's party how much he admired the one on your girlfriend."

–Zsa Zsa Gabor (1970)

The Singles Scene

In 1915, a young man wrote to noted advice columnist Dorothy Dix. He had taken his girl to dinner, to the theater and to dancing one night recently. His question was, "Should I have kissed her goodnight?" Dorothy's answer: "No, I think you did enough for her."

A certain William A. Alcott had more specific advice for unmarried men. In his *Young Man's Guide* (1849), he warned them of dangers awaiting them if they resorted to "the vice of solitary indulgence." What could befall them? Among other things:

1.) Insanity; **2.)** St. Vitus dance; **3.)** Epilepsy; **4.)** Idiotism; **5.)** Paralysis or Palsy; **6.)** Apoplexy; **7.)** Blindness; **8.)** Hypochondria; **9.)** Consumption.

"A man wants a woman first of all to be pretty, dainty...to be feminine."

–*Ladies Home Journal* (February, 1919)

In the late 1920s, Dorothy Dix counseled marriageable women to dress well and "especially learn how to dance well and to play a good game of bridge."

"An unmarried girl should not go alone on overnight trips with any young man, even with her fiancé."

–Emily Post's Etiquette (1969)

The Married Woman

Around the end of the thirteenth century, a wealthy old bourgeois of Paris wrote a helpful manual of advice for his teenage wife. He included these words to guide her whenever she left the house (chaperoned, of course):

"Keep your head high, your eyes lowered, looking neither at man nor woman, neither to the left nor right. Don't laugh or stop to speak with anybody...When you're in church, find a secret, solitary place in front of some nice altar or image and stay there, your head upright, your fine lips always moving in prayer..."

–Le Ménagier de Paris

"She is not truly delicate who uses, or endures patiently, the use in others, of those coarse, vulgar words...such as: 'My stars!' 'My soul!' 'By George!' 'Good heavens!' etc. Such expressions, besides being indelicate, savor not a little of profanity. They are exceedingly unbecoming in all, but especially females."

–*The Young Wife*, William A. Alcott (1855)

The role of the wife vis-à-vis her husband, according to winter issues of the 1948 *Ladies Home Journal*:

"Are you neat and clean when your husband returns from work? Are your meals served promptly?...Does your husband think you are a good housekeeper?...How do you compare with the wives you know...as a cook, as a housekeeper, as a companion? Do you honestly show up better than they—or as well?" (This and other magazines urge women to be consistently cheerful when hubby returns at night.)

"A man expects to support his wife. To create a comfortable and attractive home for him is her side of the bargain."

Modern women—and men—may find the following a bit more helpful:

"Make sure you never, never argue at night. You just lose a good night's sleep, and you can't settle anything until morning anyway."

–Rose Kennedy

"The first duty of love is to listen."

–Paul Tillich

Helpful Hints for Housewives

How to remove stains from clothing—a medieval solution:

For silks, satins or damasks, soak the stain in the juice of a sour or unripe acidic fruit like grape or crabapple ("verjuice").

For less delicate fabrics, apply a mixture of clean lye and ashes to the stain, let dry and rub the mixture off.

A pre-Civil War American recipe for ginger beer:

> 3 gallons water
> 3 large tablespoons ginger
> 2 pounds brown sugar
> 1 teacup good yeast

Let the mixture stand twenty-four hours, then strain it through a thick bag and bottle it. After twenty-four hours, it is all right to use.

Two tips from the Victorian era:

To preserve irons from rust, melt fresh mutton suet, smear it over the iron while hot, then dust it well with unslaked lime, pounded and tied up in muslin.

To take away freckles, boil slowly for two hours in a saucepan five cups of loose elder leaves to eight cups of rainwater. Strain, then when cold, wash the face with a cloth dipped in the liquid and let dry.

A 1911 humorist imagines engaged couples on rapid transit.

Who's the Boss?

"I would like to have engraved inside every wedding band Be kind to one another."

–Randolph Ray

Did you ever guess why dad walks his darling Mary Jane down the aisle and "gives her away"? Liberated or not, they're still repeating an ancient tradition: at the wedding a father transfers his absolute power of authority over his daughter to her new "master."

For centuries, shoes and slippers have symbolized marital authority. In early Anglo-Saxon weddings, the bride's father handed the groom one of her slippers, and according to custom, the young husband bopped her over the head with it.

In some German peasant weddings today, the fiancé presents his intended with a handsomely decorated pair of slippers, again symbolizing his mastery over her. If, during the marriage, people consider his wife the boss, they say he is "under his wife's slipper."

But watch out for foot power struggles! Today in Iran, Syria, Cyprus, Turkey, India and parts of Europe, on their wedding day—either at the ceremony or leaving the bride's house—the bride and groom will try to step on each other's toes. Whoever does it first will supposedly rule the roost.

Most modern Muslim brides will struggle—but not too hard—to step on the groom's foot before he stomps on hers. The woman will usually let her man win to prevent him from losing face before his friends.

"Men have authority over women because Allah has made the one superior to the other...As for those wives from whom you fear disobedience, admonish them, send them from your bed and beat them."

–*The Koran, Sura 4:34*

"A donkey, a woman, a walnut tree,
 The more they're beat, the better they be."

–Old English Maxim

"Thy husband is thy lord, thy life, thy keeper,
 Thy head, thy sovereign..."

–Shakespeare, *The Taming of the Shrew*

According to an old Welsh law, "a husband must not give to his wife more than three blows with a broomstick which is not longer than his arm, nor thicker than his middle finger."

In China, despite the Revolution's laws protecting wives, before a 1980 reform husbands could legally beat and torture their wives.

In 1979, when the Kenyan parliament (composed of one hundred and sixty-eight men and four women) attempted to make severe corporal punishment of wives illegal, a member of parliament argued: "It is very African to teach women manners by beating them."

In seventeenth-century England, a wife could be led to market with a halter around her neck and sold like a cow.

Marriage contracts of ancient Egypt were designed to protect women, and Egyptian wives were considered the equals of their husbands. In modern Egypt and other Muslim countries, the story is quite different...

In Saudi Arabia today, a woman who independently chooses a groom her parents and family disapprove of may be banished from their household.

But on to happier thoughts...

Honeymoon Myths and Realities

*"The bridal honeymoon should blossom into the
perfect flower of ideal marriage."*

–Th. H. Van de Velde, M.D.

Why do we call it "honeymoon"? Is it the sweetness of those first moonlit nights spent together in Aruba or the Big City? Actually, some say it comes from this old Teutonic custom: newlyweds ran off, holed up and drank *hydromel* (a fermented honey potion with a big kick to it) for thirty days, "until the moon waned."

Apparently, Attila the Hun didn't last that long. Rumor has it that, armed with gallons of *hydromel*, he drank himself to death on his wedding night.

Honeymoon trips, some historians tell us, hark back to times of marriage by capture, when a man and his newly-won bride would hide out from her parents.

In reality, the majority of the world does not enjoy the luxury of a honeymoon vacation after the wedding. In most cases, the bride immediately moves in with her husband's family, where she is expected to do a hefty share of work under the watchful eye of her mother-in-law. (Even if the couple has separate living quarters, a honeymoon trip is usually out of the question for low-income, rural populations.)

Niagara Falls became a favored honeymoon spot during the second half of the nineteenth century. It was particularly fashionable in the 1930s, when newlyweds were quick to "shuffle off to Buffalo."

Today's Orthodox Greek Wedding

"As when the welcome land
   appears to swimmers,
Whose sturdy ship Poseidon
   wrecked at sea,
Confounded by the winds
   and solid waters…
So welcome to her gazing eyes
   appeared her husband.
From round his neck she never
   let her white arms go.
And rosy-fingered dawn
   had found them weeping."

–Homer

Whether in Greece, Europe or the United States, an orthodox Greek wedding is performed as it has been for ages. Even though the couple may be officially engaged, the ceremony combines betrothal and the wedding itself. Here is how it goes, step by step:

1. At the start of the betrothal service, the priest lights two candles and hands them to the bride and groom. This symbolizes the light of Christ, a beacon to illuminate their way.

2. The priest makes the sign of the cross, in turn, over their heads. Then, three times, he declares each betrothed to the other.

3. He places the betrothal rings on the right hands of the couple, and the rings are exchanged three times to invoke the presence of the Holy Trinity.

4. Now the wedding: Joining the couple's right hands, the priest prays for their union. Their hands remain joined until the end of the ceremony. (In India, Sri Lanka and other Islamic countries, the couple's clothing may be tied together throughout the ceremony.)

5. The bride and groom are crowned as a royal couple—king and queen of their household. The priest holds two wreaths, joined by ribbons, above them and prays. Then the wreaths are interchanged three times before being worn as crowns.

6. The couple drinks wine from a common cup—a token of conjugal sharing.

7. The priest leads the couple three times around the table. All join in and dance around the altar.

An explanation of the sugar coated almonds that are served at Greek wedding receptions:

"The fresh almond has a bitter-sweet taste that is symbolic of life itself. The sugar coating is added with the hope that the life of the new family has more sweetness than bitterness. The odd number of almonds is indivisible, just as the newlyweds should remain undivided."

—From a 1991 program of a wedding at Taxiarchae Greek Orthodox Church, Watertown, Mass.

How Many Wives? How Many Husbands?

"Hogamus, higamus, men are polygamous;
Higamus, Hogamus, women monogamous."
—Old verse

"Whichever of you marries the most women is
the best Muslim."
—Kay Ka'us, 11th-century ruler
of Ziyared

Mohammed had nine wives, but when he laid down his marriage laws he only allotted four apiece to his followers.

Polygamy, that age-old practice of taking multiple spouses, still exists today. We find it in Islamic cultures, in Africa, the South Pacific, the Himalayas, the Far East and elsewhere. In most cases, polygamists are men with more than one legal wife (*polygyny*). It's much rarer to find female polygamists with several husbands (*polyandry*)—but we'll get to that later.

Modern experts estimate that, at present, 25% of men in West African societies have two or three wives. In some Nigerian villages, it's over 50%, and elsewhere the figure is higher.

In Nepal, it's legal to take several wives, provided you can support them all. In countries like Pakistan and Saudi Arabia, polygamy is now largely restricted to those cases where a first wife is barren. A 1960 law abolished polygamy in Vietnam but, illegal or not, Vietnamese men are still practicing it.

On August 4, 1991, in Malaysia, Islamic Religious Department Director Mohamad Saad Mehamad urged women to allow their husbands to take up to four wives, for two reasons: 1) to prevent extramarital affairs; and 2) to help marry off single women. (There are now more than sixty thousand unmarried women over the age of thirty in peninsular Malaysia alone.)

Men like the Bantu of Tanzania continue to accumulate two or three wives, largely in order to acquire a more numerous, family work force. They achieve status too, since generally the more wives a man has the more important he appears to others (and to himself).

In the Trobriand Islands of Papua, New Guinea, the more mates a man has the richer he becomes, thanks to the yam tribute that comes with his wives. (These days, polygamy over there is restricted to a select few, notably the Paramount Chief.)

Elsewhere, however, polygamy can become too expensive a sport to indulge in at the present time. In Pakistan, for instance, only a few landlords and *mullahs* outside the city can afford it. Besides that, the very wealthy Pakistani are now too Westernized to do it.

How do wives fare in a polygamous marriage? The worst scenario is when multiple wives are housed under the same roof. That happened more in the past than today. On the bright side, the first wife—as furious as she could be about sharing her husband—at least got to boss the new ones around.

But unless the man was wealthy, the last female to arrive usually wound up with loads of dirty work and had to babysit for the others.

These days, marrying a polygamous man doesn't usually benefit a woman economically. If he is four times wealthier than most men, he can afford four times as many wives, so any financial benefits will probably be split four ways.

As for the men, polygamy can get pretty messy at times. Take, for example, a place like the Comoro Islands, located off the coast of Madagascar. There, a married couple customarily lives in the wife's parents' home (and you can forget about bringing a second wife to live there). That means a polygamous husband has to support more than one household...

Now this system has some advantages: If the husband has to travel on business to some faraway place, he can have a nice little *pied-à-terre* there, entertaining local business acquaintances at his second home and developing a wider network of contacts.

BUT CAUTION! Male polygamists are supposed to deal evenhandedly with all their wives, and this, my friends, is easier said than done. Here is what one expert has to say about it:

"A man with two wives is in trouble. Every day he has to perjure himself to keep peace between them, because there is always constant jealousy among co-wives. If he buys them a gift, he can't divide it in front of them or he'll have a real problem.

"And he can't eat a full meal at one house, because when he goes to the other and isn't hungry there will be trouble. As for sleeping arrangements, he has to share them equally. If he sleeps more with one wife, the other will complain to her parents...

"The customary treatment of two wives should be thoroughly taught to a man, or he should read about it in books. If he doesn't there will be perpetual problems."

–Mtoro bin Mwingi Bakari
(see Ottenheimer, *Marriage in Domoni*, 1985)

What about women with multiple mates (*polyandry*)? It's less common than men with plural wives (*polygyny*), but it still occurs in the 1990s. In the mountains of Tibet, a herdsman will share his wife with his brothers or half-brothers. That way they don't have to divide the family estate or their collective earnings from the yak herd.

Next question: who gets the little woman on which night? The eldest brother has the final say on that, so let's hope he's a good lover. (Ladies! Interested in a trip to Tibet? Send one dollar and a stamped self-addressed envelope...)

Polygamy, U.S.A.

"Take a new wife every year, friend, since a used calendar is really not much use."

—Persian poet Sa'di, 13th century

Nineteenth-century Mormon elders took several wives, convinced that it was part of their religion. When the government passed a law against the practice in 1862, the Mormon women themselves organized to protest the ruling.

In March of 1863, Mormon leader Brigham Young was arrested for bigamy. His case never came to trial.

Threatened with the loss of their church and property, the Mormons finally decided to obey the law of the land and condemn polygamy. So after 1890, all known Mormon polygamists were excommunicated.

But today the plural wife system is still going strong among splinter group Mormons. Many of them have taken to the hills of Arizona, notably to Colorado City (nicknamed "Cohab Canyon" by U.S. marshals).

Law enforcement officials estimate the number of current Utah polygamists at thirty thousand. They believe another twenty thousand have set up house in Montana, Arizona, Wyoming, California and other states.

Though polygamy is an embarrassment to law abiding Mormons, it has some definite pluses for excommunicated patriarchs, above and beyond the delights of a harem. To wit:

In agricultural communities, polygamous marriages create more children to help work the land.

Some polygamous husbands achieve status by controlling the distribution of their own young wives (often only twelve and thirteen years old) to other men.

And some can get rich too...

In 1985, Utah authorities discovered that 65-year-old John Ortell Kingston's wives had defrauded the government out of millions of dollars. They had collected state and federal welfare benefits, claiming they were unwed, abandoned mothers. Apparently the whole family became wealthy thanks to food stamps, Social Security payments and other federal funds.

As for the harem, polygamist Tom Green explained on TV in 1988 that his fridge door had a monthly schedule posted on it, stipulating which of his four wives shared the conjugal bed on which night.

$\mathscr{A}$ Tale of a Wife With Three Husbands

Alma Schindler was no polygamist, for she wed her men at different times, after legal divorces or widowhood in between. But two things make Alma's case interesting: 1) she married eminent figures (composer Gustav Mahler, architect Walter Gropius, writer Franz Werfel); and 2) her conjugal exploits were celebrated in song by the incomparable Tom Lehrer.

Alma

The loveliest girl in Vienna
Was Alma—the smartest as well,
Once you picked her up on your antenna
You'd never be free of her spell.

Her loves were many and varied
From the day she began her beguine,
There were three famous ones whom she married,
And God knows how many between.

> Alma, tell us—
> All modern women are jealous—
> Which of your magical wands
> Got you Gustav and Walter and Franz?

The first one she married was Mahler,
Whose buddies all knew him as Gustav,
And each time he saw her he'd holler,
"Ach, that is the *freulein* I must have!"

Their marriage, however, was murder.
He'd scream to the heavens above,
"I'm writing *Das Lied von der Erde*,
And she only wants to make love."

> Alma, tell us—
> All modern women are jealous—

You should have a statue in bronze
For bagging Gustav and Walter and Franz.

While married to Gus she met Gropius,
And soon she was swinging with Walter.
Gus died, and her tears were copious;
She cried all the way to the altar.

But he would work late at the Bauhaus
And only came home now and then.
She said, "What am I running—a chowhouse?
It's time to change partners again."

Alma, tell us—
All modern women are jealous—
Though you didn't even use Pond's,*
You got Gustav and Walter and Franz.

* At the time this was written, magazines featured cold cream ads with photos of debutantes and the slogan: "She's engaged, she's lovely, she uses Pond's."

While married to Walt she met Werfel,
And he, too, was caught in her net.
He married her, but he was careful,
'Cause Alma was no Bernadette.

And that is the story of Alma,
Who knew how to receive and to give.
The body that reached her embalma
Was one that had known how to live.

> Alma, tell us—
> How can they help being jealous?
> Ducks always envy the swans
> Who get Gustav and Walter,
> You never can falter
> With Gustav
>> And Walter
>>> And Franz.

–Tom Lehrer

A Potpourri of Wedding Trivia

"The amount of women in London who flirt with their own husbands is perfectly scandalous. It's simply washing one's clean linen in public."

–Oscar Wilde

The phrase "tying the knot" comes from the ancient Celtic *handfasting* ceremony in which the bride and groom were literally bound together at the hands. This knot-tying allowed couples to pledge their troth for one year and a day at a time. After that, they could part, if mutually agreed.

According to an old Michigan law, a married couple had to live together or be imprisoned.

Queen Victoria's wedding cake was three yards wide and weighed three hundred pounds.

Queen Elizabeth topped that in her 1947 marriage to Prince Philip. Twelve wedding cakes were presented to her. The one she cut at her wedding reception measured nine feet tall, weighed five hundred pounds and arrived in a large van accompanied by two motorcycle escorts.

A Shinto wedding in Japan now includes the new custom of a lavishly decorated, western-style wedding cake. Since such cakes can be incredibly expensive, most commercial wedding palaces supply cardboard reproductions of the real thing. But ersatz or not, wedding couples delight in the cake-cutting ceremony.

In America today, a TV soap opera wedding can attract more viewers than a presidential address. Small wonder then that producers don't mind spending over $20,000 per day for fresh flowers (they wilt fast under the glaring lights) and at least as much for wedding gowns and formal suits.

It used to be customary among North American eskimos for the bride and bridesmaids to warm up the bridegroom's bed on the wedding night. If invited by the groom, some bridesmaids could spend the night in the nuptial bed provided they not fool around with him.

Couples in America, Japan and other countries are marrying later these days than a few generations ago. Average age at U.S. nuptials: twenty-four for brides; twenty-six for grooms.

Traditionally, in villages located in Rwanda and Tanzania, on the day of their wedding the bride and groom faced one another, each seated on the lap of an elderly woman.

A Pueblo Indian groom moves into the home of his bride's parents. If the marriage turns stormy, it's the man who leaves and goes home to mother.

Cape Codders say that last century in the Truro-Provincetown region, couples couldn't marry until they had planted beach grass to help prevent dune erosion. (And you thought ecology was a new invention.)

In present-day Egypt, after the successful signing of a marriage contract, the bride's mothers and sisters let out a high pitched Indian war whoop. They also whoop at the cutting of the wedding cake.

Each year, the Hilton Semiramis in Cairo invites back all couples married in that hotel the preceding year, on the condition that they wear their wedding dress. That, of course, can pose a problem for expanding expectant mothers.

At wedding receptions in Bali, the bride holds up a cloth in front of the groom, who strikes it through with a dagger, obviously indicating a successful penetration of the bride.

In India, when a professional is called in to decorate the bride's hands with henna, the designs are thought to replace the lavish jewels that once might have adorned the betrothed. These days, elaborate flowers are painted on her hand and around her fingers to form rings.

Those brilliant nose rings worn by Indian women are simply for decoration these days. Up to a generation ago, however, a woman wore a ring in her nose to show that she was married. Initially, this was a large gold hoop; later on, a smaller one.

The Asmat people of New Guinea believe that, in order to have a baby, a woman must be impregnated by the spirit of an ancestor and the spirit is always of the same sex as the newborn child.

Since the Asmat keep their masculine and feminine activities totally separate, the women raise their daughters, while their husbands take charge of the sons as soon as they're weaned.

The Punan of Borneo maintain that women are born without a soul and don't acquire one until marriage time. This belief has one interesting advantage: since Punan girls are without souls, they can't be blamed for sinning, so they lead a pretty active sex life.

Now a Punan woman can't be wed until she actually does get a soul, and it's up to her future husband to find one for her. How? He simply goes off on a head-hunting expedition. After returning with his booty, the soul from the severed head is transmitted to the bride in a ceremony that can last several days. The captured head is tied to the head of the bride, and the medicine man performs various rites until he's certain that the soul has been successfully transferred.

In case you're wondering about all those massacres, the Punan will assure you they only do it for spiritual reasons. Besides, how else could they get married?

This is how the very first household was set up, according to a legend of the Diola people in West Africa:

First man on earth wanted to cuddle with first woman. First woman refused. Preferred to stay alone. Woman hollowed out hole in ground to hide in. Rains came and water filled hole. Then first man made thatched roof over woman for rain-proof hut. First woman liked it a lot, so she stayed and cuddled with first man forever.

And finally, why on earth do people fall hopelessly in love and marry? Here is how Plato explained it in the *Symposium*:

Originally, the Master of the Gods created human beings as hermaphrodites, with two heads, four arms, four legs, etc., and two sexes all in one. But these creatures became so powerful that their Creator, fearing their strength, sliced them in half—into male and female, as we are now.

Ever since then each human being, sensing it is incomplete, keeps searching for its other half until it finally discovers the right one, combines with it, and becomes whole at last.

❤ ❤ ❤ ❤ ❤ ❤

"Love, be true to her; Life be dear to her;
Health, stay close to her; Joy, draw near to her,
Fortune, find what you can do for her,
Search your treasure-house through for her,
Follow her footsteps, the wide world over,
And keep her husband always her lover!"

—Old English Toast

❤ Anniversary Gifts ❤

<u>Year</u>	<u>Gift</u>
1	Paper
5	Wood
10	Tin, Aluminum
15	Crystal
20	China
25	Silver
30	Pearls
40	Rubies
45	Sapphires
50	Gold
60	Diamonds

Broom Jumping, Then and Now

"Seen my lady home las' night,
Jump back, honey, jump back."

–Paul Laurence Dunbar

In the United States, "jumping the broom" dates back to nineteenth-century slave marriages on southern plantations. Here's how it came about:

American slaves weren't legally entitled to a Christian wedding ceremony. Although a white or black minister (or the plantation owner himself) did perform a religious ceremony at slave marriages, it wasn't binding under the law. And it couldn't include the words "Till death do us part," since plantation masters had the power to part man and wife—and, unfortunately, some did, when it was in their interests.

So the slaves invented their own ceremony, with bride and groom jumping over a broom—the broom being the symbol for home in certain parts of Africa. This jumping was done in high spirits, sometimes with the claim that whoever got over the broom first, or higher or without stumbling would be boss of the household.

The white master's family, especially the women, organized weddings of their slaves, often devoting great energy and care in the preparations. They were usually held on weekends or at Christmas, so family and friends of both colors could be present. Until the Civil War and the abolition of slavery, broom jumping remained a lively feature of the slave marriage celebration.

♥ ♥ ♥ ♥ ♥ ♥ ♥ ♥

Today, nearly a century-and-a-half later, "broom jumping" is coming back into fashion among African-Americans. This is part of a growing trend to incorporate African-Caribbean and American slave traditions into modern black weddings.

The Always and Forever Wedding Chapel in Detroit, for instance, now furnishes couples with Yoruban priestesses to perform ancient African rites at their weddings. Other African and Caribbean sources provide them with Caribbean black cakes, wedding rings engraved with hieroglyphics, African-style wedding invitations, imported African designs for wedding gowns and dinner jackets made of African *kente* cloth.

As for the American slave heritage, the newly-founded Imperial Broom Company of Richmond, Virginia sold one thousand colonial-style brooms during

151

a recent six-month period to couples wanting to "jump the broom" at their weddings.

Marriage Makes the News

"There are only about 20 murders a year in London and not all are serious—some are just husbands killing their wives."

–H. Hatherhill, Commander, Scotland Yard, *News Summaries* (1954)

Just before the editor of the *South Carolina Fountain Inn Tribune* stopped publishing his paper in the early 1950s, he decided to surprise his readers with a wedding description to knock them off their feet. Here it is, as reprinted forty years later in Ann Landers' column:

"The groom is a popular young bum who hasn't done a lick of work since he got kicked out in the middle of his junior year at college. He manages to dress well and have plenty of spending money because his dad is a soft-hearted fool who covers the kid's bad checks instead of letting the rotter go to jail where he belongs.

"The bride is a skinny little idiot who had been kissed and handled by every boy in town since she was 12 years old. She smokes cigarettes in secret and drinks corn liquor when she is out joy-riding in her dad's car at night. She cannot cook, sew or keep house.

"The groom wore a rented dinner suit over athletic underwear of imitation silk. His pants were held up by pale green suspenders. His patent leather shoes harmonized nicely with the axle grease in his hair.

"The bride wore some kind of white thing that left most of her legs sticking out at one end and her bony back sticking out the other. The young people will make their home with the bride's parents, which means they will sponge off the old man until he dies, and then she will have to take in washing...

"Postscript: This may be the last issue of the Tribune, but my life's ambition has been to write up a wedding and tell the unvarnished truth. Now that it is done, death can have no sting."

♥ ♥ ♥ ♥ ♥

Offbeat weddings—shades of the '70s—have come back in style in the '90s. A newspaper article by Judith Gaines (*Boston Globe*, August 22, 1993) recorded weddings on a roller coaster, in an auto parts store, during a sky diving free fall and in a lion's cage. It also told what happened when a New York couple had a flock of doves released at the end of the marriage ceremony. Instead of flying around the room the stubborn birds "roosted on the overhead chandeliers and would not come down—to the consternation of the guests, who were peppered with their droppings during the seated dinner."

You've seen descriptions of other unconventional weddings in the papers and on TV: pet weddings, cemetery weddings, nudist weddings, underwater weddings...the list goes on. One Massachusetts justice of the peace officiated last year at a Halloween costume marriage ceremony and will soon do one in a butterfly atrium, surrounded by hordes of free-flying butterflies. (Let's hope they are better behaved than the doves.)

❤ ❤ ❤ ❤ ❤

Item from the *New York Times* (October 10, 1993): At a wedding in a SoHo art gallery the bride was laughing so hard and continuously through the ceremony that the woman marrying them finally stopped the service to ask if the groom was tickling her. "No," answered the bride, "If I didn't laugh my teeth would chatter."

❤ ❤ ❤ ❤ ❤

Dear Abby:

I'm eighty-four years old, but I still like the ladies. My wife is the jealous type, and she never wants me to leave the house without her because she's afraid I might call on an old girlfriend, so she hides my false teeth.

What should I do?

Grandpa Max

Dear Grandpa:

Your wife is looking out for your best interests. She wants to make sure you don't bite off more than you can chew.

Abby

–Abigail Van Buren, 1981

Roses and Jasmine at a Javanese Wedding Party

"Bird to nest from wandering wide; Happy bride-groom, seek your bride."

–Alfred Edward Housman (1859-1936)

A 1990s wedding celebration in Java is a magic time machine rolling us back to graceful and picturesque rituals of centuries past. This party is the most visible feature of the union of man and wife in Java and always the highlight of the occasion.

The event doesn't take place, however, until a week after the marriage itself. That week includes a three-day separation between bride and groom—a time for spiritual cleansing and contemplation. (Many Thai grooms go to a Buddhist monastery during a similar period of marital segregation.)

A Javanese wedding reception is usually held in a commercial wedding hall brimming with flowers and the strains of Indonesian music. Melodies are rendered by a *gamelan* orchestra, a unique blend of drums, gongs and wood or metal chimes.

The stars of the event, the bride and groom, take center stage (and are sometimes literally up on a stage), resplendent in brightly colored, finely decorated *sarongs*. These expensive *sarongs*, like those of some guests, are often rented for the occasion.

❤ ❤ ❤ ❤ ❤

Some details from a recent wedding party in Java:

The bride and groom wear matching *sarongs* of vibrant green, embroidered with gold and silver thread. The groom is barechested, his *sarong* reaching up to just below his breast (of course the bride's garb modestly covers hers). Both of their costumes are finished off with silver belts, saffron-colored roses and trailing jasmine. The young man wears a green *fez*, and his bride is adorned with a snood-shaped headdress, a combination of woven gilded leaves, jasmine and assorted flowers. Dark-colored triangular shapes, dyed on her forehead and outlined in gold leaf, indicate that she is a virgin.

Throughout the party, guests approach the bridal couple to wish them well. They are dressed in *sarongs* and silk jackets, and some of the males wear strips of batik cloth around their heads. As they near the bride and groom, they keep their palms and fingers together, aligned in a prayer position, with the fingertips pointed slightly upwards and toward the couple. The newlyweds welcome each guest with their hands in an identical prayer position, touching fingertips to fingertips as one visitor after another wishes them joy and a happy marriage.

The guests have come armed with their wedding presents, each trying to outdo the other in lavishness of offerings. In turn, members of the bridal party hand out favors and gifts to them, along with food to take home (such eats, however, are usually inedible, after being lengthily displayed unrefrigerated).

The bridal party itself is a visual feast, with one group in gold-hued *sarongs*, another in matching lavender ones, and yet another in pink or orange. The color indicates their function at the reception, such as distributing favors or guiding guests to the large buffet.

Meanwhile, as if the occasion were not memorable enough, every aspect is recorded by professional photographers.

(From information provided by the author's sister Edith after her recent attendance at a wedding party in Jakarta.)

❤ ❤ ❤ ❤ ❤

At other Javanese wedding celebrations you may witness the following long-lived customs:

The couple each take three rolled-up betel leaves and throw them at one another for good luck.

They feed each other three times from the same plate of rice for union and a fertile marriage.

The groom crushes a raw egg with his bare foot (symbolizing fertility), and then the bride lovingly washes it off his foot with a pitcher of water (symbolizing—you guessed it—female submission).

An Irreverent Marriage Medley

"Many a man in love with a dimple makes the mistake of marrying the whole girl."

–Stephen Leacock

Vignettes

A wife was having no luck dealing with her chronic drunk of a husband. One night when he returned home in a boozy stupor, she decided to change her tactics and give him tender, loving care instead of lectures:

WIFE: Sit down, dear, and I'll stroke your forehead and sit on your lap.

HUSBAND: Sure, I may's well. I'll get hell anyhow when I get home.

♥ ♥ ♥ ♥ ♥

Sadie's husband, Jake, disappeared one day. She went down to the police station with a friend and made a missing person's report. Her friend was astonished to hear Sadie describe Jake as a handsome Adonis, tall, dark, young and gorgeous:

FRIEND: Sadie, excuse me, but with the description you gave them, they'll never find Jake.

SADIE: So who wants him?

❤ ❤ ❤ ❤ ❤

A son received news that his father had died overseas. Overcome with grief, he sent a wire: "WHAT WERE FATHER'S LAST WORDS?"

The answer came: "FATHER HAD NO LAST WORDS. MOTHER WITH HIM TO THE END."

❤ ❤ ❤ ❤ ❤

Rita had set her cap for Ron, the man of her dreams. When he invited her out to dinner, she was in ecstacy. As she floated on cloud nine, the waiter approached:

WAITER: How would you like your rice, baked or sauteed?

RITA: Thrown.

❤ ❤ ❤ ❤ ❤

Mrs. Vandervere gave instructions to a painter starting to do her portrait:

"I don't own many jewels, but please paint some into the portrait. Show me wearing a triple-strand pearl necklace (make it look genuine, of course), a smashing emerald and pearl bracelet, diamond and pearl pendant earrings set in platinum and, oh yes, platinum rings with large precious stones."

"But Mrs. Vandervere," said the painter, "You obviously don't care much for jewelry. Why do you want all that in the painting?"

"Because if I die before my husband does I want his next wife to go nuts trying to find where all those jewels are hidden."

❤ ❤ ❤ ❤ ❤

SOUTHERN BELLE: Mother, what do you give a man who has everything?

MOTHER: Encouragement.

168

From Bed to Verse

"As Thomas was cudgel'd one day by his wife,
He took to his heels and fled for his life.
Tom's three dearest friends came by in the squabble,
And saved him at once from the shrew
        and the rabble,
Then ventured to give him some sober advice—
But Tom is a person of honor so nice,
Too wise to take counsel, too proud to take warning,
That he sent to all three a challenge next morning.
Three duels he fought, thrice ventured his life,
Went home, and was cudgeled again by his wife."
                                        –Jonathan Swift

A word to husbands:

"To keep your marriage brimming,
 With love in the loving cup,
 Whenever you're wrong, admit it;
 Whenever you're right, shut up."
                                        –Ogden Nash
(From *Marriage Lines: Notes of a Student Husband*)

Limericks

"There once was an old man of Lyme,
Who married three wives at a time;
When asked, 'Why a third?'
He replied, 'One's absurd!
And bigamy, sir, is a crime.'"

"A lady from Boca Raton
Bought a gift for her dear hubby, Don.
He said, 'Show it to me,'
Answered she: 'Nosiree!
But I'll wear it for you later on.'"

"One Perfect Rose"

"A single flow'r he sent me, since we met.
All tenderly his messenger he chose,
Deep-hearted, pure, with scented dew still wet—
One perfect rose.

I knew the language of the floweret,
'My fragile leaves,' it said, 'his heart enclose.'
Love long has taken for his amulet
One perfect rose.

Why is it no one ever sent me yet
One perfect limousine, do you suppose?
Ah, no, it's always just my luck to get
One perfect rose."

–Dorothy Parker

The following verses from a nineteenth-century ballad are probably not an early harbinger of women's lib, but a tongue-in-cheek spoof of all-too-independent ladies:

"I'll be no submissive wife
  No, not I; no, not I
  I'll not be a slave for life
  No, not I; no, not I...

"Should a humdrum husband say
That at home I ought to stay
Do you think that I'll obey,
Do you think that I'll obey?
No no no no no no no
No no no, not I."

–Alexander Lee (1835)

Four Fictional Proposals

Jack Worthington goes under the name Ernest when he vacations in the country—as a sort of escape. He meets Gwendolen in the country, falls in love with her and proposes to her. Unfortunately, Gwendolen seems more enamored of the name Ernest than of Jack himself:

JACK: But you don't really mean to say that you couldn't love me if my name wasn't Ernest?
GWENDOLEN: But your name is Ernest.

JACK: Yes, I know it is. But supposing it was something else? Do you mean to say you couldn't love me then?

GWENDOLEN (*glibly*): Ah! That is clearly a metaphysical speculation, and like most metaphysical speculations has very little reference at all to the actual facts of real life, as we know them.

JACK: Personally, darling, to speak quite candidly, I don't much care about the name of Ernest...I don't think the name suits me at all.

GWENDOLEN: It suits you perfectly. It is a divine name. It has a music of its own. It produces vibrations.

JACK: Well, really, Gwendolen, I must say that I think there are lots of other much nicer names. I think Jack, for instance, a charming name.

GWENDOLYN: Jack?...No, there is very little music in the name Jack, if any at all, indeed. It does not thrill. It produces absolutely no vibrations...The only really safe name is Ernest.

JACK: Gwendolen, I must get christened at once—I mean we must get married at once. There is no time to be lost.

GWENDOLEN: Married, Mr. Worthing?

JACK (astounded): Well...surely. You know that I love you, and you led me to believe, Miss Fairfax, that you were not absolutely indifferent to me.

GWENDOLEN: I adore you. But you haven't proposed to me yet. Nothing has been said at all about marriage. The subject has not even been touched on.

JACK: Well...may I propose to you now?

GWENDOLEN: I think it would be an admirable opportunity. And to spare you any possible disappointment, Mr. Worthing, I think it only fair to tell you quite frankly beforehand that I am fully determined to accept you.

JACK: Gwendolen!

GWENDOLEN: Yes, Mr. Worthing, what have you got to say to me?

JACK: You know what I have to say to you.

GWENDOLEN: Yes, but you don't say it.

JACK: Gwendolen, will you marry me? (Goes on his knees)

GWENDOLEN: Of course I will, darling. How long you have been about it! I am afraid you have had very little experience in how to propose.

JACK: My own one, I have never loved any one in the world but you.

GWENDOLEN: Yes, but men often propose for practice. I know my brother Gerald does. All my girl-friends tell me so. What wonderful blue eyes you have, Ernest! They are quite, quite blue. I hope you will always look at me just like that, especially when there are people present...

-From *The Importance of Being Earnest* by Oscar Wilde

❤ ❤ ❤ ❤ ❤

Sophia Western's father has been listening at the door while Tom Jones proposes to his daughter. Liking Tom, Western is furious that Sophia has coyly told her beloved suitor to wait a whole year before they marry. He bursts in the room and gives her an angry earful. This is what follows:

"What would my Papa have me do?" cries Sophia.

"What would I ha' thee do? says he, "why [give him] thy hand this moment.

"Well, Sir" said Sophia, "I will obey you.—There is my hand, Mr. Jones."

"Well, and will you consent to [have him] to-morrow morning?" says Western.—

"I will be obedient to you, Sir," cries she.

"Why then tomorrow morning be the day," cries he.

"Why then to-morrow morning shall be the day, Papa, since you will have it so," says Sophia.

Jones then fell upon his knees and kissed her hand in an agony of joy, while Western began to caper and dance about the room, presently crying out,— "Where the devil is Allworthy? He is without now, talking with that d—-d lawyer Dowling when he should be minding other matters."

He then set out in quest of him, and very opportunely left the lovers to enjoy a few minutes alone.

-From *Tom Jones* by Henry Fielding

❤ ❤ ❤ ❤ ❤

One of the most extroardinary proposals in print comes from *The Young Visiters*, a novel of adult life and love created in the early twentieth century by a nine-year-old girl called Daisy Ashford.

Our hero, Bernard, has just given a "rat-tat" at heroine Ethel's door. Here is what follows—the climactic, heavy breathing love scene (with Daisy's original spelling and punctuation):

"Be quick cried Bernard I have a plan to spend a day near Windsor Castle and we will take our lunch and spend a happy day.

"Oh Hurrah shouted Ethel I shall soon be ready as I had my bath last night so wont wash very much now.

"No dont said Bernard and added in a rarther fervent tone through the chink of the door you are fresher than the rose my dear no soap could make you fairer.

"Then he dashed off very embarrassed to dress.

Ethel blushed and felt a bit excited as she heard the words and she put on a new white muslin dress in a fit of high spirits. She looked very beautifull with some red roses in her hat and the dainty red ruge in her cheeks looked quite the thing. Bernard heaved a sigh and his eyes flashed as he beheld her and Ethel thought to herself what a fine type of manhood he represented with his nice thin legs in pale broun trousers and well fitting spats and a red rose in his button hole and rarther a sporting cap which gave him a great air with its quaint check and little flaps to pull down if necessary. Off they started the envy of all the waiters.

"They arrived at Windsor very hot from the jorney and Bernard at once hired a boat to row his beloved up the river. Ethel could not row but she much enjoyed seeing the tough sunburnt arms of Bernard tugging at the oars as she lay among the rich cushons of the dainty boat. She had a rarther lazy nature but Bernard did not know of this. However he soon got dog tired and sugested lunch by the mossy bank.

178

"Oh yes said Ethel quickly opening the sparkling champaigne.

"Don't spill any cried Bernard as he carved some chicken.

"They eat and drank deeply of the charming viands ending up with merangs and choclates.

"Let us now bask under the spreading trees said Bernard in a passiunate tone.

"Oh yes lets said Ethel and she opened her dainty parasole and sank down upon the long green grass. She closed her eyes but she was far from asleep. Bernard sat beside her in profound silence gazing at her pink face and long wavy eye lashes. He puffed at his pipe for some moments while the larks gaily caroled in the blue sky. Then he edged a trifle closer to Ethels form.

"Ethel he murmered in a trembly voice.

"Oh what is it said Ethel hastily sitting up.

"Words fail me ejaculated Bernard horsly my passion for you is intense he added fervently. It has grown day and night since I first beheld you.

"Oh said Ethel in suprise I am not prepared for this and she lent back against the trunk of the tree.

"Bernard placed one arm tightly round her. When will you marry me Ethel he uttered you must be my wife it has come to that I love you so intensely that if you say no I shall perforce dash my body to the brink of yon muddy river he panted wildly.

"Oh dont do that implored Ethel breathing rarther hard.

"Then say you love me he cried.

"Oh Bernard she sighed fervently I certinly love you madly you are to me like a Heathen god she cried looking at his manly form and handsome flashing face I will indeed marry you.

"How soon gasped Bernard gazing at her intensly.

"As soon as possible said Ethel gently closing her eyes.

"My Darling whispered Bernard and he seiezed her in his arms we will be marrid next week.

"Oh Bernard muttered Ethel this is so sudden.

"No no cried Bernard and taking the bull by both horns he kissed her violently on her dainty face. My bride to be he murmered several times.

"Ethel trembled with joy as she heard the mistick words.

"Oh Bernard she said little did I ever dream of such as this and she suddenly fainted into his out stretched arms.

"Oh I say gasped Bernard..."

–From *The Young Visiters* by Daisy Ashford

💜 💜 💜 💜 💜

And now, the pièce de résistance: Mehitabel the Cat receives and accepts a marriage proposal. Mehitabel—who believes in the transmigration of souls and is convinced she was once Cleopatra—has hitherto refused to commit herself to wedded life. But now at last she looks favorably upon a certain tomcat's offer. The tale is typed by Archy the Cockroach, who can't manage the shift key or punctuation:

> its wrong for an artist to marry
> a free spirit has gotta
> live her own life
> about three months ago along came a
> maltese tom with a black heart and
> silver bells on his neck and says
> mehitabel be mine
> are you abducting me percy i asks him
> no said he i am offering marriage
> honorable up to date
> companionate marriage
> listen i said if its marriage
> theres a catch in it somewheres
> ive been married again and again
> and its been my experience
> that any kind of marriage
> means just one dam kitten after another
> and domesticity always ruins my art

but this companionate marriage says he
is all assets and no liabilities
its something new mehitabel
be mine mehitabel and i promise
a life of open ice boxes
creamed fish and catnip
well i said wotthehell kid
if its something new i will take a
chance theres a dance or two
in the old dame yet
i will try any kind of marriage once
you look like a gentleman to me percy
well archy i was wrong as usual...

–From *The Lives and Times of Archy and Mehitabel*
          by Don Marquis

$\mathscr{A}$ Salem Witch Wedding

"Let me live 'neath your spell
To do that voodoo that you do so well…"

–Cole Porter

Witches are alive and well and living in America today. In fact, an estimated four thousand of them continue to practice their arts in Salem, Massachusetts, alone. Fortunately, they are not satanic demons. Instead, like that sweet sorcerer Glinda in *The Wizard of Oz*, these present-day witches use their powers for the good of all. And lately their benign witchcraft has become increasing popular in New England revivals of old-fashioned witch weddings.

Even if you're not a witch, their brand of marriage ceremony may appeal to you. But before you try it out, you must be sure to consult an astrologer in order to choose the most auspicious time and place for your wedding.

According to Laurie Cabot, the official witch of Salem, this is what you will witness at a modern witch wedding:

"[A magic circle nine to thirteen feet in diameter] is formed of nosegays, flowers and ribbons. The immediate family and other Witch friends stand just inside the circle and form an inner circle around the altar, which is draped in pink, white or black cloth. Frankincense and myrrh are burning, two chalices filled with wine or spring water stand between one white and one black candle. Next to the chalices are the two wedding rings..."

–From *Power of the Witch* by Laurie Cabot (1989)

Enter the main cast: An assistant priestess makes her appearance with two nine-foot black silk cords draped around her neck. She leads the bride and groom into the magic circle from a northerly direction. When they are inside it, a high priestess casts a charm on the circle with a magic wand. The bride and groom walk around the circle, greeting four invisible archangels in each quarter of the area as they pass by. At that point, the assistant "sweeps" the circle with a magic broom, in order to brush away all the wrong things that have happened in the couple's previous lives.

Then the couple kneels on pillows before the altar, facing each other, and the high priestess and her assistant use their occult powers to "charge" the rings and chalices, imbuing them with a spiritual power.

And now comes the high point of the ceremony, the actual tying of the knot, or "handfasting"—a custom inherited from the ancient Celts. After the bride and groom declare their mutual love and their goals in marriage, each one picks up the other person's wedding ring and drops it into the other's chalice. While their hands are crossed, holding the chalices, the assistant priestess binds them loosely with her black silk cords in a sort of figure eight. The bride and groom then sip wine or water from each other's chalice. After that the remaining liquid is poured into a bowl, the rings are removed from the empty chalices and placed on their fingers. The high priestess raises the loose cord above their heads, then binds the knot tightly, saying: "I tie the knot."

Finally, she hands one end of the cord to each of the couple and, as they hold the cord between them, she places one hand on each of their heads, saying before all present: "You are both bound in infinity. So mote it be." The wedding gifts are "charged," the circle is opened, and all now joyfully celebrate the marriage.

So ends the modern witch's wedding. You see, it's not one bit scary—and a darned sight cheaper than nuptials at the Ritz.

Love Letters to Husbands, Wives and Fiancés

"If kisses could be sent by mail, Madame,
You would read my letter with your lips."

–E. Rostand, Cyrano de Bergerac

Napoleon Bonaparte to his wife, Josephine, from a military campaign in Italy (March 30, 1796):

"I haven't spent one day without loving you. I haven't spent one night without holding you in my arms. I haven't taken one cup of tea without cursing the self-respect and ambition that keep me apart from my very soul.

"In the midst of operations, whether leading the army or inspecting the camps, my adorable Josephine takes up all my heart, occupies my mind, absorbing my thoughts.

"If I go away from you with the speed of the Rhone's torrent, it is to be able to see you again more quickly. If I get up to work in the middle of the night, that is because it might speed up the arrival of my sweet by a few days."

Here Napoleon scolds Josephine for addressing him coldly as "vous" in her letter, rather than using the more intimate "tu":

"You horrible thing, how could you have written that letter!...And then between the 23rd and the 26th there are four whole days. What were you doing since you didn't write to your husband!

"Ah! my friend, that *vous* and those four days make me regret my past indifference to you. Woe to whoever's behind this. As punishment and torture may he suffer what any proof of his pleasure would make me suffer. Hell hath no greater punishment. Nor furies, nor serpents. 'Vous!' 'Vous!' Ah, what will become of me in two weeks?...

"Farewell, woman, torture, happiness, hope and soul of my life, whom I love, whom I fear, who inspires tender feelings in me, making me one with Nature, along with impetuous impulses as volcanic as thunder.

"I ask neither eternal love nor fidelity from you, but only *truth*, utter frankness. The day you tell me 'I love you less' will be the last day of my love and of my life.

"If my heart were base enough to love without being loved in return, I would tear it apart with my teeth.

"Josephine, Josephine! Remember what I've told you: Nature has given me a strong and decisive character. She has made you out of lace and gauze. Have you stopped loving me?...

"P.S.: The war is unbelievable this year. I've distributed meat, bread, fodder. My armed cavalry will soon be on the march. My soldiers are showing me amazing confidence. You alone make me miserable. You alone, the pleasure and torment of my life. Here's a kiss for your children who you don't write a word about. Good Lord! that would make your letters longer by half: your visitors wouldn't have the pleasure of seeing you at 10:00 A.M. Woman!!!"

❤ ❤ ❤ ❤ ❤

Robert Browning to Elizabeth Barrett a few days before their elopement (September 13, 1846):

(Early in the letter Browning explains to his beloved that he wishes his past behavior toward her had been worthy of his deepest feelings for her.)

"...Words can never tell you, however,—form them, transform them anyway,—how perfectly dear you are to me—perfectly dear to my heart and soul.

"I look back, and in every one point, every word and gesture, every letter, every *silence*—you have been entirely perfect to *me*—I would not change one word, one look—

"My hope and aim are to preserve this love, not to fall from it—for which I trust to God, who procured it for me, and doubtlessly can preserve it.

"Enough now, my dearest, dearest, own Ba! You have given me the highest, completest proof of love that ever one human being gave another. I am all gratitude—and all pride...that my life has been so crowned by you.

"God bless you prays your very own

R"

Elizabeth Barrett to Robert Browning (September 13, 1846):

"My own beloved, if ever you should have reason to complain of me in things voluntary & possible, all other women would have a right to tread me underfoot, I should be so vile & utterly unworthy. There, is my answer to what you wrote yesterday of wishing to be better to me...you!—What could be better than lifting me from the ground & carrying me into life & the sunshine?...All that I am, I owe you—if I enjoy anything now & henceforth, it is through you. You know this well. Even as *I*, from the beginning, knew that I had no power against you..."

♥ ♥ ♥ ♥ ♥

John Jay Chapman, American poet, to his Wife, Minna (September 21, 1891):

"I have sealed up each one of these letters thinking I had done—and then a wave of happiness has come over me—remembering you—only you, my Minna—and the joy of life. Where were you, since the beginning of the world? But now you are here, about me in every space, room, sunlight, with your heart and arms and the light of your soul—and the strong vigor of your presence. It was not a waste desert in Colorado. It is not a waste time, for you are here...

"This is a love letter, is it not? How long is it since I have written you a love letter, my love, my Minna? Was the spring hidden that now comes bubbling up overflowing curb and coping-stone, washing my feet and my knees and my whole self?..."

Here Chapman regrets time spent in useless discussions or quarrels:

"How diligently have we set fact to fact and consideration against consideration during the past years—as if we were playing dominoes for our life. How cloudy I have been—dragging you down, often nailing useless nails, cutting up and dissecting, labeling, crucifying small things—and there was our great love over us, growing, spreading—I wonder we do not shine—or speak with every gesture and accent giving messages from the infinite—like a Sibyl of Michel Angelo. I wonder people do not look after us in the street as if they had seen an angel."

Heloise to Abelard (Twelfth Century):

What romance could be more moving than the true experience of Abelard and Heloise and what love letters more soul-searing than Heloise's to Abelard, whom she addresses as her "lord, father, husband and brother"?

Briefly, here is their story:

In medieval France lived Abelard, the most famous philosopher-teacher in Paris...brilliant, handsome, charming, and sought-after. One day, he decided to add to his list of conquests 17-year-old Heloise, known far and wide for her intelligence and talents (and twenty years his junior).

Heloise's uncle and guardian, Fulbert, immediately accepted Abelard's request to become Heloise's tutor and naively gave the man complete control over her during lesson periods. The young girl submitted willingly, learning more about life than literature in the process. She soon became pregnant and secretly gave birth to a child. Unfortunately, her uncle Fulbert found out and, naturally, flew into a rage. The couple got married in Fulbert's presence but kept their wedding secret in order not to damage Abelard's career.

Then the tragic ending. One night Fulbert, still angry with Abelard and deeply suspicious of him, sent hired thugs to his quarters with orders to castrate him. The horrible deed done, Abelard retired to a monastery and arranged for Heloise to become the head of a convent outside of Paris. There Heloise yearned in vain for a word of love or consolation from Abelard. And from there she penned him these lines:

"...You know, my beloved, and everyone knows that in losing you I lost everything. The shameful and public treachery that snatched you away from me in one terrible blow also robbed me of myself. Much more than the loss of you, it is how I lost you that pains me so. And the greater my sorrow, the greater the consolation needs to be. In any case, the only person who could console me is you, the source of all my unhappiness...

"I have meekly accomplished everything you commanded. Rather than upsetting you, with one word from you I found the courage to ruin myself.

"But I did something even more astounding! My love became delerium: with no chance of ever recovering it I sacrificed the only object of this love. On your orders...I took on another costume and another soul...I proved to you that you were the sole master of my heart as well as my body...

"It is you alone I wanted, never your possessions. I never thought of bridewealth nor my pleasures or desires, only of satisfying you. The title 'wife' was deemed more sacred and strong; 'Mistress,' however, seemed sweeter to me and—may it not shock you— even 'concubine' or 'prostitute.' I thought that the humbler I made myself for you, the more grateful you would be and the less I would hamper your destiny...

"Consider, I beg you, what I am asking you: it's so little and so easy to do. I am deprived of your presence— at least write to me—a letter is so simple for you—the sweetness of your own image..."

Abelard did write back to Heloise: long sermons crammed full of moral and religious advice—with nary a tender word. Heloise had the good grace not to trash his letters but, tragic figure or not, his preachy discourses are definitely banned from this book.

❤ ❤ ❤ ❤ ❤

From *The Dream and the Business* by John Oliver Hobbes:

"I love you so much and so completely that now I believe in marriage. You must be more than mine—you must be mysteriously, and legally, and eternally, and respectably, mine. If there were no marriage service, my instinct would invent it."

The Poets on Love and Marriage

"Marriage is intimate to the degree of being sacred."

–William O. Douglas

"On the hill top a jewelled path shines fair,
   On the back of her skirt are stitched phoenixes
      male and female.
   On the two sleeves of her mantle are seen a pair
      of crows.
   Now fold up her gauze clothes and put them in
      the clothes box."

–On undressing the Bride
(from an old Chinese ballad)

"At Katushika the river water
Runs gently, and the plum blossom
Bursts out laughing.
The nightingale cannot withstand so many joys
And sings, and we are reconciled.
Our warm bodies touch,
Cane branch and pine branch."

–Japanese love song

"Make thee another self for love of me,
That beauty still may live in thine or thee."

–William Shakespeare (1564–1616)

"If ever two were one, then surely we,
If ever man were lov'd by wife, then thee,
If ever wife was happy in a man,
Compare with me ye women if you can...

Then while we live, in love let's so persever,
That when we live no more, we may live ever."

–Anne Bradstreet (ca. 1612–1672)

"She half enclosed me with her arms,
  She press'd me with a meek embrace;
And bending back her head, look'd up
    And gazed upon my face.

'Twas partly love, and partly fear,
  And partly 'twas a bashful art,
That I might rather feel, than see,
    The swelling of her heart.

I calm'd her fears, and she was calm,
  And told her love with virgin pride;
And so I won my Genevieve,
    My bright and beauteous Bride."

                    –Samuel Taylor Coleridge (1772–1834)

"If thou must love me, let it be for naught
  Except for love's sake only. Do not say
  'I love her for her smile—her look—her way
Of speaking gently,—for a trick of thought
That falls in well with mine...'
But love me for love's sake, that evermore
Thou may'st love on, through love's eternity."

                    –Elizabeth Barrett Browning (1806–1861)

"Now folds the lily all her sweetness up,
And slips into the bosom of the lake.
So fold thyself, my dearest, thou, and slip
Into my bosom and be lost in me."

–Alfred Lord Tennyson (1809–1893)

"Raise me a dais of silk and down;
    Hang it with vair and purple dyes;
Carve it in doves and pomegranates,
    And peacocks with a hundred eyes;
Work it in gold and silver grapes,
    In leaves and silver fleurs-de-lys;
Because the birthday of my life
    Is come, my love is come to me."

–Christina Georgina Rossetti (1830–1894)

Bibliography

Alcott, William A., *The Young Wife*, 1855.

Bahadur, K. P., *The Castes, Tribes and Culture of India*, Vol. 7, 1981.

Bailey, Beth L., *From Front Porch to Back Seat*, 1988.

Baker, Margaret, *Wedding Customs and Folklore*, 1977.

Barth, Fredrick, *Balinese Worlds*, 1993.

Beidelman, T.O., *The Kaguru*, 1971.

Bhutto, Benazir, *Daughter of Destiny*, 1989.

Bloxham, Christine G., and Picken, Molly, *Love and Marriage*, 1990.

Busch, Ruth C., *Family Systems*, 1990.

Chenevière, Alain, *Vanishing Tribes*, 1986.

Corin, James, *Mating, Marriage and the Status of Women*, 1910.

Christopher, Robert C., *The Japanese Mind*, 1983.

Clare, Anthony, *Lovelaw: Love, Sex and Marriage Around the World*, 1986.

Cross, Mary, *Egypt*, 1991.

De Coppet, Ed., *Understanding Rituals*, 1993.

Diamant, Anita, *The New Jewish Wedding*, 1985.

Dragadze, T., *Kinship and Marriage in the Soviet Union*, 1984.

Edwards, Walter, *Modern Japan Through its Weddings*, 1989

Ellis, Havelock, *Sex and Marriage*, N.Y., 1952.

Fricke, Thomas E., *Himalayan Households*, 1986.

Gabor, Zsa Zsa, *How to Catch a Husband*, 1970.

Genovese, Eugene, *Roll Jordan Roll*, 1976.

Good, Anthony, *The Female Bridegroom*, 1991.

Hammer, Ellen, *Vietnam Yesterday and Today*, 1966.

Kane, Harnett, *Dear Dorothy Dix*, 1952.

Kern, Stephen, *The Culture of Love*, 1992.

Kerns, Virginia, and Brown, Judith K., *In Her Prime*, 1992.

Lamb, David, *The Africans*, 1987.

Lee, Vera, *The Reign of Women in 18th-Century France*, 1975.

Lerner, Laurence, *Love and Marriage*, 1979.

Linklater, Andro, *Wild People*, 1990.

Lipsell, Linda Otto, *To Love and to Cherish*, 1989.

Mackey, Sandra, *The Saudis*, 1987.

Mernissi, Fatima, *Beyond the Veil*, 1975.

Murphy, Brian, *The World of Weddings*, 1978.

Ndekezi, Sylvestre, *Rituel du mariage coutumier à Rwanda*, 1984.

Ottenheimer, Martin, *Marriage in Domoni*, 1985.

Le Ménagier de Paris, Slatkine Reprints, s.d.

Post, Elizabeth, *Emily Post's Etiquette*, 1969.

Randall, Rona, *The Model Wife, Nineteenth-Century Style*, 1989.

Reingold, Edwin M., *Chrysanthemums and Thorns*, 1992.

Russell, Bertrand, *Marriage and Morals*, 1929.

Scher, Paula, *The Honeymoon Book*, 1981.

Seligson, Marcia, *The Etermal Bliss Machine*, 1973.

Shaban, Bouthaina, *Both Right and Lefthanded: Arab Women Talk About Their Lives*, 1991.

Shorter, Aylward, *East African Societies*, 1974.

Spence, Jonathan D., *The Search for Modern China*, 1990.

Tasker, Peter, *The Japanese*, 1987.

Tober, Barbara, *The Bride: a Celebration*, 1984.

Tomasevic, N., and Djuric, R., *Gypsies of the World*, 1988.

Turner, Geoffrey, *Indians of North America*, 1992.

Urlin, Ethel, *A Short History of Marriage*, 1969.

Van der Velde, Dr. Th. H., *Ideal Marriage*, 1968.

Van Pelt, P., *Bantu Customs in Mainland Tanzania*, 1982.

Visser, Margaret, *The Rituals of Dinner*, 1991.

Westermarck, E.A., *A History of Human Marriage* (3rd vol.), 1922.

Weston, Mark, *The Land and People of Pakistan*, 1992.

Wheaton, Barbara Ketcham, *Savoring the Past*, 1983.

Wilson, W. Emerson, *Plantation Life in the Diaries of Martha Ogle Forman*, 1976.

Some Useful Journals: *National Geographic, China Quarterly, American Ethnologist, Far Eastern Economic Review, Journal of Comparative Family Studies, Signs, Middle East Studies, Ladies Home Journal, Women's Home Companion, Modern Bride*.

ABOUT THE AUTHOR

Vera Lee has authored eight books and articles in areas such as literary criticism, social history, cooking and contemporary theater.

Formerly Chairman of Boston College's Romance Language Department and Executive Director of the French Library in Boston, she has been awarded the Palmes Academiques from the French Ministry of Education. She recently served as a panelist for the National Endowment for the Humanities.